"When we run into the inevitable 'bumps and bruises' in our relationships, what do we do? Do we assert our rights and try to convince others why and how we've been wronged—or do we turn to God's Word for guidance? In this wise and down-to-earth book, Brian Noble lays out a Christ-centered framework for effectively working through conflict and, ultimately, experiencing true peace with those around us."

Jim Daly, president of Focus on the Family

"I'm deeply grateful for Brian's love for the gospel and his commitment to promoting biblical peacemaking in the body of Christ! I pray God uses this book to guide many people to step onto the path of peace."

Ken Sande, author of *The Peacemaker* and founder of Relational Wisdom 360

"Winsome as always! Brian is a clear and compelling communicator about how the gospel of Jesus Christ sets us free to face conflicts and tensions in our lives. His practical, insightful, and inspiring book is a great addition to peacemaking and is a must-read for all of us!"

Judy Dabler, president of Creative Conciliation

"Brian Noble offers a clear pathway for Christians to turn everyday conflict into opportunities for peace. He writes with vulnerability and humility as one who has engaged and embodied reconciliation and has more than just mastered the facts. Readers will be challenged to examine and interpret their personal story through God's grace and practical principles of peacemaking."

Jim Van Yperen, founder and president of Metanoia Ministries and author of *Making Peace: A Guide to Overcoming Church Conflict*

"I've known Brian as a peacemaking colleague for years, but I didn't *really* know him until reading this book. He demonstrates both humility and transparency, with his personal accounts making this book very relatable. To say Brian is passionate about peacemaking can't be overstated, and his passion rings through in these pages. You will find in this book a useful approach to pointing people to true peace. To quote Brian,

'Peace is possible if, at first, you connect with the Peacemaker himself.'"

Dwight Schettler, president of Ambassadors of Reconciliation

"As long as I have known Brian, he has embodied peacemaking. This book beautifully captures years of his personal and professional reconciliation experience. In a compelling and accessible format, filled with poignant stories and practical advice, Brian skillfully walks anyone experiencing relational tension on a journey back toward connection. *The Path of a Peacemaker* provides a biblical framework for how lasting peace is established as we examine our own stories in light of the gospel."

Daniel Teater, LPC, MDiv, MAC, CCC, president of Live at Peace Ministries

"*The Path of a Peacemaker* describes Brian Noble's unique approach for resolving conflict. Brian not only imparts ideas with illustrations but also tells his own story, weaving it throughout. In sharing his own weaknesses, Brian exemplifies walking *The Path of a Peacemaker*. Readers are encouraged to walk the path to Jesus and with him in their conflicts, relying on his justice and mercy. Many will be blessed by this book."

Ted Kober, senior ambassador for Ambassadors of Reconciliation

"This book is worth its weight in gold! Brian Noble shares a compassionate journey that can help anyone transform tough problems into positive solutions for genuine, healthy relationships. Each chapter in *The Path of a Peacemaker* is filled with solid, practical navigation for conflict resolution, as if Jesus were standing in our midst. Brian Noble lays out three bold steps to 'ascend, reflect, and connect' using our life stories and a renewed perspective about God. *The Path of a Peacemaker* should be on everyone's required reading list to better understand how our perspective about God affects the peace we have in everyday relationships."

Judy Steidl, COO of ICC Peace

THE PATH OF A
PEACEMAKER

YOUR BIBLICAL GUIDE TO HEALTHY
RELATIONSHIPS, CONFLICT RESOLUTION,
AND A LIFE OF PEACE

P. BRIAN NOBLE

BakerBooks

a division of Baker Publishing Group
Grand Rapids, Michigan

Published by Baker Books
a division of Baker Publishing Group
PO Box 6287, Grand Rapids, MI 49516-6287
www.bakerbooks.com

Printed in the United States of America

Library of Congress Cataloging-in-Publication Data
Names: Noble, P. Brian, 1974– author.
Title: The path of a peacemaker : your biblical guide to healthy relationships,
    conflict resolution, and a life of peace / P. Brian Noble.
Description: Grand Rapids : Baker Publishing Group, 2019.
Identifiers: LCCN 2018045148 | ISBN 9780801094293 (pbk.)
Subjects: LCSH: Conflict management—Religious aspects—Christianity. |
    Interpersonal relations—Religious aspects—Christianity. | Peace—Religious
    aspects—Christianity.
Classification: LCC BV4597.52.C58 N63 2019 | DDC 261.8/73--dc23
LC record available at https://lccn.loc.gov/2018045148

19 20 21 22 23 24 25   7 6 5 4 3 2 1

To my wife, Tanya, and kids,
who have helped me grow and become
the peacemaker I am today.

To Pastor Kent, who provided me
the time to pursue my passion.

CONTENTS

INTRODUCTION

Got conflict? You're not alone. Whether within your family, your church, your workplace, or your sphere of friends, peace can sometimes be an elusive thing. I know firsthand. The nonprofit organization I direct, Peacemaker Ministries, is immersed in the goal of helping people find peace amid conflict. In that role, I see my share of conflict—and reconciliation.

But I've also got a life of my own. So besides my professional perspective, I have a personal perspective on conflict and peace. Like you and everyone else, I have a story—and mine was once nothing *but* conflict. Over the years, I've seen God work in amazing ways. I've had the privilege of seeing peace come out of conflict not just as someone who leads seminars and workshops and biblical counseling sessions but also as someone who's experienced God's power in his own life.

For more than thirty-five years, Peacemaker Ministries has equipped and assisted Christians and their churches to respond to conflict from a biblical perspective. I've seen friendships restored, marriages restored, churches restored, schools restored, entire communities restored. But most significantly, I've seen the man staring at me in the mirror each morning restored.

This book blends the experiences of other people and my own. Vulnerability, I believe, is a strength, not a weakness. It is one thing to preach the virtues of God from a distant theoretical standpoint; it is quite another to speak from the perspective of having seen your own life changed by his power.

When this happens, conflict turns into peace, frustration into clarity, and turmoil into unity. Ultimately, God is glorified. We can rejoice in our newfound hope, strength, and vision. So join with me as we look at what God has done, can do, and will do as we faithfully follow his Word.

In part one, "Tension," we will discover underutilized, improperly utilized, and properly utilized tension. We will go into depth about tension in our everyday lives. God has used tension to refine and develop his followers for centuries. That is why we can consider it all joy when we encounter various trials.

In part two, "Story," we will see that we all have a story that is running internally. From that story we develop our perspective. Every story has context, and that context will determine how we will respond to conflict. Think about your life as a book: we never know what chapter we enter in someone else's book, and they do not know what chapter they enter in our book. That is why discovering our story and expanding our perspective are so important when we are experiencing tension or conflict.

In part three, "Ascend," we will get up and go back to biblical core values. We will think about the men and women of old and the parables Jesus told: Noah was asked to build, so he built. Abraham was challenged to believe, so he believed; then he was challenged to sacrifice, so he sacrificed. Moses was called to lead, so he led. Deborah was appointed to judge, so she judged. Ruth was faithful, and she became God's instrument to save his people. Jeremiah was created to prophesy, so he did. Jonah was called to evangelize a nation; he fled to avoid his calling, and then things got fishy (God put him back on track). Jesus told a story of a younger son who finds himself in the pigpen of life; then he came to his senses and headed back to his father to repent. Here is what all these people have in common: they operated out of a desire to obey God. When we are in conflict, we want our interactions to flow through God's Word and be filtered by God's Spirit. Returning to biblical core values will help us glorify God, bring him the attention he deserves, and ultimately bring us peace.

In part four, "Reflect," we will see that once we have reset our mind on God and his Word, it is time to humbly reflect. Our time of reflection is simple but ultimately the most difficult. It is simple in that we look through the lens of the gospel. It is the most difficult because, through our fallenness, it is hard to see our own blind spots (I guess that is why they are called "blind spots"). Together we will look at four tools that will help us view ourselves rightly. We will ask the Holy Spirit to reveal to us our contribution to the conflict.

In part five, "Connect," we will evaluate how to connect with those with whom we are in conflict. Humility is key to this reconnection. I like to say this: "When humility steps into the room Jesus wins." However, humility does not come naturally, nor does it come easily. Our fallenness will do whatever it takes to avoid humility. Remember, when you face the greatest injustice, you are the most Christlike. We will discover how to have a productive conversation with those with whom you have conflict, and we will close by looking at forgiveness.

In part six, "Conclusion," we will look beyond the process we've discussed to what comes after. Sometimes, despite our best efforts, things simply do not go very well. What do we do then? We will be reminded of the importance of living God's one-another principles. Ultimately, we must remember Romans 12:18: "If possible, so far as it depends on you, be at peace with all men."

PART 1
TENSION

1

The World Is One Tense Place

*I have never met a man who has given me as much trouble
as myself.*

Dwight L. Moody

Though it was more than thirty years ago, I remember
the moment clearly. I was living with my mother and
sister in a dinky apartment in Grandview, Washington, so
named because of its magnificent views of Mount Adams.
My view of life wasn't nearly so magnificent.

On an April evening in 1981, seven candles glowed on my
birthday cake. My mother sat across from me, trying hard to
pretend things were normal. My sister sat next to me. And
there was an empty chair next to her. That's where my father
would have been sitting before the divorce, before my mother
had left my father and we'd moved from a nice house to a
cramped apartment. The split was no less devastating to me
than when Mount Saint Helens, 110 miles to the west, had

erupted the previous year in the deadliest volcanic eruption in US history.

"Make a wish," my mother said, a hopeful half smile on her face.

Big Wheel? Transformers? G. I. Joe action figure?

Nope. All I wanted for my birthday was my dad to come back, my family to be whole again, and my life to have some sense of security in a world where I felt so little safety. At the time, I couldn't have put my feelings into words, but I think what I really wanted was peace in a personal world full of dawn-to-dusk tension.

The divorce turned my world upside down. In the late 1970s and early '80s, divorce wasn't common. In fact, in the small town in which I was raised, I don't think any other kids in my class had parents who were divorced. So the problem wasn't just that I missed having my father around but also that kids made fun of me. I was the odd duck. I was different. I was different enough to begin with—uncoordinated, poor eyesight, no confidence. My parents' divorce was salt in a gaping wound as I entered middle school.

During my elementary school days, I was labeled a "special kid" because I struggled in school. In third grade, we all lined up to have our eyes checked. My heart beat faster the closer I got to the front of the line. Finally, it was my turn.

"Which way is the *E* pointing?" the school nurse asked.

"Uh, I don't see an *E*," I said. "I only see a black square."

My teacher intervened. "Now, you quit being funny, Mr. Noble, and tell her which way the *E* is pointing."

I gulped. "Honest, I only see a black square."

"Step closer," said the nurse.

When I was about a foot from the eye chart, I saw the huge *E*.

I can remember the first time I saw leaves on a tree after getting glasses. I saw with clarity and felt comfort. Dogs used to scare me a lot—I couldn't see them. But I could *feel*. And what I mostly felt was tension.

Back when my parents were first divorced, I spent one week at my mom's house and one week at my dad's. My sister and I would take our suitcases on the bus each Friday so that we'd have stuff to take to the other parent's house after school. The bus driver was nice enough to tuck them away so we didn't have to be quite as embarrassed, though it's pretty hard to hide the fact that you're bouncing from parent to parent like a Ping-Pong ball.

We did this back-and-forth gig for five years before my mother decided it wasn't working. I was twelve, my sister was fourteen, and we had to choose which parent we wanted to stay with. My sister chose our dad. I chose our mom. Until I chose Christ, this was the biggest decision I'd ever made in my life.

"Mom, why did you leave Dad?" I would ask her from time to time after I went to live with her.

She always deflected the question the same way: "I love you, and I love your dad." I was giving her every opportunity to say what she wanted to say about the man, but she only repeated that she loved me and she loved him.

Much of my childhood was a blurry memory. And, really, who could blame me? Who would want to remember a childhood like I had? All I really remember was a dad who was hurt, kids at school who made fun of me, and staring into the flames of those seven birthday candles, wishing for some peace in my life.

Tension—It's Everywhere You Look

Sorry, I hope you don't feel dumped on. But part of understanding peace is being real with one another in a world that likes to sweep uncomfortable stuff under the rug. So I'm going to be real with you, and I hope you'll be real with yourself. Here is a great place for the two of us to start, with the understanding that we live in a world that's taut with tension.

Look around. Tension is everywhere. Maybe you experience it at the breakfast table with the spouse you chose and who chose you but who now seems like your enemy at times. Maybe you experience it with the neighbor who sticks political candidate signs in their lawn two months before the election and, if the person wins, leaves those signs up for months afterward just to rub it in. Maybe you experience tension with your boss, who plays you like a puppet and, when you do something to make them look good, never bothers to say thanks.

Welcome to our tense, tense world.

Tension crackles on the political level. There is tension between Democrats and Republicans. Each party's leaders disagree among themselves on the direction their own party should be going. And, of course, there's tension between voters and politicians when voters see politicians put their own needs first.

Business partners experience tension, and it can destroy relationships and friendships. Not enough success with regard to the bottom line can create tension. Ironically, so can too much success.

Get married, and you'll experience tension. Your spouse wants Chinese food, and you want a hamburger. Your spouse wants you to fix up your house with the aplomb of Chip and Joanna of TV's *Fixer Upper*, but you prefer to spend your time watching football and to keep your money safely in a money-market account earning interest. Your spouse wants to have a baby, and you don't.

So let's say you have that baby. Maybe two or three. From their first scream, what do they create? Hey, you're catching on! Tension. They grow up. They demand time, energy, money, wisdom—stuff that, at times, can be in short supply. More tension.

You could always stay single, right? Surprise! Tension is alive and well in singleness. There's pressure from parents to meet that significant someone; pressure from friends who are constantly wanting to set you up with just the right person; pressure from within, because maybe when you made birthday wishes when you were young, you always wished for that one special soul mate; or pressure from a society that subtly considers single people damaged goods.

Maybe you think going to church will solve your problems. News flash: there's tension at every church. Church boards can be full of tension. So can the relationship between a congregation and its pastor. Maybe church members feel they hired the pastor to do ministry, but the pastor believes their job is to equip the congregation to do ministry. Differences in philosophy can cause tension. Differences in expectations can cause tension. Differences in favorite parking spots can cause tension.

So you turn your focus from the fallible work of people to the infallible work of God as seen in the Bible. But wait. There's tension in the Bible. Everywhere you look, people in the Bible are discontent. The Israelites are whining. Locusts are attacking. The authorities are throwing hard-core believers like Paul into prison.

Some Scripture passages emphasize one truth, and other passages emphasize another. I'm tense even suggesting this—you might claim I'm a heretic—but it's true: everyone has their pet doctrines. It's why we have so many denominations. And, yes, there is tension within those denominations—and tension within the churches that leave those denominations because of the denominational tension.

Beyond the Bible and church and pastors and elders and boards, maybe you can have a tension-free one-on-one relationship with God. Sorry. Still not a tension-free zone. Who among us, with a certain degree of tension, hasn't shaken an angry fist at God? We can love God and give our lives to God and follow God, but guess what? Doing so won't lead to a tension-free life. In fact, following God can *cause* tension. Suddenly, some of your friends and family members and work colleagues think you've gone off the deep end. You pray for something and it doesn't happen, which causes tension. You see a Christian you look up to not acting in a Christlike way; that creates tension.

Why? Because tension is not only out there but also in here—inside you.

Tension—It's Even inside You

Think about the last diet you went on. You wanted to be healthy, but when offered a cupcake at a colleague's going-away party, you gobbled it down like a beggar out of a Charles Dickens novel. Why? Deep down you desired pleasure and, in the tension between pleasure and resisting, saying yes to being a chocolate mess won out.

The desire for purity and holiness is inside you, but the lust of the eyes is also real, creating tension within you. You know you want to walk with God, but something takes over again and again.

Tension lurks in your thoughts. Think about the last thought you had toward yourself. What was it? Did you experience tension? Did the thought create a bridge between you and whatever you were trying to accomplish, or did it create a chasm between the two?

Tension reverberates in your emotions. Have you ever felt like crying and yelling at the same time? Marriage and kids can bring many mixed emotions. One moment you can experience joy and the next minute sadness.

All of this might have you saying, "Man, life's a bummer. Tension is everywhere. I'm doomed." Lest I leave you with such feelings of hopelessness, let me clue you in on a secret that is foundational to this book. While tension can work against you, it has a phenomenal flip side. The same tension that can so easily work against you can also work *for* you. When tension is used wisely, it can bring out the best in you and in your life.

I know this for two reasons. First, I've spent fifteen years leading and teaching peacemaker training to tens of thousands of people in multiple countries and in almost every state. I have seen tension work for good in thousands of people. And, second, through the grace and power of God, I've seen tension turn a scared, insecure, tense, timid, depressed, and pity-party young man into an adult who's confident, content, and at peace—me.

21

Am I perfect? Nope. Like everyone else, I have my moments. But instead of being that kid who thought the *E* on the eye chart was a black block, I now see clearly through the eyes of Christ. And when I blow out my birthday candles (well over forty on my last cake), I do so with expectations that transcend the unclear, unpeaceful days of my youth.

As you'll learn soon enough, we each have a story. You know the first part of mine. Let me share the rest of my story as a means of showing you the positive side of tension.

2

Tension Can Be Positive

Fiery trials make golden Christians.
Charles Spurgeon

By age twelve, I was regularly stealing Jack Daniel's whiskey from my parents. Not that I drank all that much. But that changed in 1992 when I left home and moved to Spokane, in northeast Washington, to attend a tech school. I was eighteen and lonely. My closest connection was to my mom back home. But I had no close friends, no family nearby, no Jesus. I'd heard of him; my father had taken me to church on occasion. But to be honest, when I was eighteen, Jesus meant nothing to me.

I got a job as a cook, the best perk of which was the ability to easily steal liquor from the restaurant's bar. Within six months, I was drunk more often than not, hopeless, and seriously considering killing myself. Tension doesn't get much worse than when it is causing you to consider whether to live or die.

One day I was so drunk that I passed out in class. Later, at home, I fell to my knees in desperation. "God," I said, "if you're real, show yourself to me."

No lightning bolts. No heavenly angels. No choir singing hallelujah hymns. Instead, the oddest of nudges came to my booze-blurred brain: *Quit your job, Brian.*

Huh? I had no idea why or how this idea came to me, nor did it seem like a particularly inspiring response for a help-me-or-else plea. From my perspective, my job was about the only thing I had going for me. Whatever. I quit my job. When a school counselor called me a few days later, I assumed it was either to expel me or to put me on probation for having passed out in class because of my drinking. Instead, she offered me a job.

"I know you already have one," she said, "but I have this other job I would like you to consider."

The job entailed working in a warehouse shipping products, Monday through Friday. The schedule would allow me to go to church. My grandma had sent me a birthday card in which she had listed the addresses of several local churches. She had encouraged me to try one out.

"I'll take it," I said to the counselor.

She didn't know I had just quit as a cook.

I lied in my interview, though I had no idea why. "I'm a Christian," I said, "and I need to have Sundays off so I can go to church." The statement didn't represent any sort of newfound spiritual depth; I was just playing the cultural-Christian game. My would-be employer said that wasn't a problem; the office was closed on Sundays.

For reasons beyond me, I started going to a church. It turned out the pastor had known my grandfather, who had also been a pastor. I'd never known my mom's dad; he'd died before I was born. But the pastor assumed that since my grandma had told me to attend his church and that my grandfather had been a pastor, I must be a Christian.

"Brian," he said, "let's get you involved in serving God's people."

Before I knew it, I was teaching Sunday school in front of a bunch of kids. But that didn't work out too well; I knew less about God than the kids did. So the pastor had me drive the church van to pick up kids to go to church. I loved it.

One day in the spring of 1993, I went to our youth minister, who had become a friend.

"I'm freaked out," I said. "I don't know if I'll go to heaven when I die."

"Why don't you know? Isn't Jesus your Lord?"

"Not that I know of."

"Haven't you prayed and asked Jesus into your life?"

"Sure, when I was a kid."

"But he's not your Lord?"

"I don't think so."

"Do you want him to be?"

"Sure."

I said yes to Jesus and proclaimed my faith, in water baptism, in front of hundreds of people at church.

A woman I knew ran a prison ministry. Given my past, she thought I had a great testimony to share with the inmates and encouraged me to do so. I did. Every month I went to the county jail and shared how I had been delivered from sin and how they, too, could be set free. Many inmates came to know Jesus.

Meanwhile, I started seeing changes in my life. I went from being totally insecure to being totally secure (sometimes even arrogant, though that's another story I'll share later). I started having hope. I started loving people. I started attending Bible school at my church.

I went to Bible college. I did a three-year internship. I became a pastor. I became a husband. I became a father. I earned a master's degree in 2014. And I began presenting workshops around the country and around the world on finding peace in the middle of conflict, which begins with understanding that tension is both friend and foe.

Tension as a Positive Force

Tension is usually considered a bad thing. And, often, it is. But it's also the thing that creates the energy to get well, to mend fences, to start anew. It can be a force for incredible good. Tension can make us laugh, create friendships, force us to drop our airs and become real with God. In my case, a tension so strong I almost took my own life became a desperation to turn that life around—after people reached out to me.

The desire to be successful can be a good tension. This tension can drive us to achieve goals we never thought possible. It can provide the energy we need to wake up in the morning. But such tension can also create a desire that gets out of control.

The desire to be liked is mostly good tension. The desire to like others is excellent tension. If nobody cared whether others liked them or if nobody cared about liking others, our world would be a miserable place. Many people believe we live in the most selfish time in history. That may be true, but there's still a remnant of likability tension. Just go to Facebook and click "Like."

Being challenged is good tension. When we're challenged, we learn and grow and get stronger. Consider weight lifting. When you lift a barbell, the action creates tension that can be painful during the process, but the end result is strength.

So you get the idea. Tension can bring out the worst in us. Tension can bring out the best in us. If ignored, tension is essentially useless to us. I can't think of a better example to explain tension than something first patented in England on March 17, 1845: the rubber band. Like the tension in a rubber band, tension in life can be used in two ways.

Tension can be used in healthy ways. Properly utilized tension is *useful*. For example, a rubber band can bind together a dozen pencils. It can help a little girl create a ponytail. It can seal an opened bag of potato chips to keep them fresh. It can power a model airplane into the sky.

Tension can be used in unhealthy ways. Improperly utilized tension is *dangerous*. Held between two fingers and stretched back, a rubber band can be snapped to intentionally hurt a sibling. (Not, of course, that I know this from personal experience!) Stretched back from the thumb, it can be shot at a fellow student during class. (Ditto.) Wrapped too tightly around a wrist or a finger, a rubber band can cut off circulation.

If a rubber band is simply cast aside, it creates, in essence, unutilized tension. Unutilized tension is *irrelevant*—unused potential for good. True, such tension isn't doing anyone any harm. But why wouldn't we want to exploit something that has the potential to help us? In the same way, why wouldn't we want to use the tension in our lives to be more for God than we might otherwise be?

So Then What Is Tension?

Peacemakers' definition of tension is simple: being stretched or strained. Tension is a motivating factor for change—in an array of arenas. Consider the earth. Beautiful mountains were formed by compressional tension. Large gaps in the earth's surface, like the Grand Canyon, were formed by the tension created by water.

Amazing, huh? Tension can result in beauty. But, of course, tension can also result in destruction. Tension in the earth causes earthquakes. Closer to home for me, tension led to the volcanic eruption of Mount Saint Helens.

Likewise, in life, tension plays out in diverse ways. Let's check out a few.

Motivational tension. Tension can motivate you to take action. The tension of being overweight can motivate you to diet and exercise. The tension of wanting to be an excellent athlete can motivate you to practice. The tension of wanting success can motivate you to work hard. Tension used in healthy ways is powerful. But the same tension can lead to negative results. You are overweight, so you get stressed out and depressed. You are athletic, but you become jealous of others' abilities and talents. You want success, so you step on everyone else to achieve that success. Tension used in unhealthy ways is powerful.

Relational tension. Tension within a relationship can produce a best friend or a worst enemy. Think of friendships based on trust and love; when tension enters the relationship, the friendship grows. But often when tension takes the form of a disagreement, an expression of differences, poor communication, or some other event, an enemy is made.

Here's an example of relational tension called "Don't be that person." I'm sure you have met them. Who are they? That person has many characteristics. They are someone who

sits with their arms crossed and stares at people

interrupts others when they try to talk

polarizes by asking others to take sides

debates every detail while not listening to others' input

says, "Yeah, yeah" when someone else shares an idea

is not teachable

opposes others internally but pretends they approve

selfishly uses resources to benefit only themselves

crushes ideas during brainstorming

smiles with their mouth but kills with their eyes

Whew. Are you that person? In many ways, I once was. Tension can pull us away from the things that matter or push us toward those very things.

Marital tension. The burning desire for your spouse caused you to get married. You were in love. The tension of singleness, of loneliness and the need for purpose, moved you to say, "I do." You looked your spouse in the eyes and saw the good, the not so good, and the very good. Then something happened. The honeymoon ended, and you experienced a different tension. One person wanted to focus on work, and one desired to focus on family. Words were said, arguments exploded, and problems ensued.

Below are some other types of tension:

Spiritual tension: your walk with God is stretched or strained.

Parenting tension: your relationships with your children are stretched or strained.

Sibling tension: your relationships with your siblings are stretched or strained.

Church tension: your church relationships are stretched or strained.

Workplace tension: your professional relationships are stretched or strained.

Leadership tension: your leadership roles cause you to be stretched or strained.

Educational tension: your relationships within an educational environment are stretched or strained.

Self-tension: your own self is stretched or strained from within.

Until we truly understand the tension that leads to conflict, we are ill-equipped to overcome unhealthy tension or conflict. What better place to begin to understand than the Bible?

3

Tension Is Biblical

Were it not for tribulation I should not understand the
Scriptures.

Attributed to Martin Luther

Your children are at each other's throats. Your employees are about to mutiny. Your church members have taken sides over the dismissal of an associate pastor. Relax, you're not the first person to feel some tension. Tension even appears in the Bible. Remember Cain and Abel? They were the children of Adam and Eve, and the tension was thick between them, so thick, in fact, that after God counseled Cain to control his "countenance," he "rose up against Abel his brother and killed him" (Gen. 4:8). If God is your personal counselor and you respond to that counsel by murdering your brother, you're experiencing some serious tension.

Tension is so prevalent in the world that the Bible says creation groans: "For we know that the whole creation groans and suffers the pains of childbirth together until now" (Rom. 8:22). If you let it, the tension of the world can overwhelm you. But if the Bible is full of tension that works against peace and contentment, it also brims with hope that tension can work *for* peace and contentment.

Consider Proverbs 27:17: "Iron sharpens iron, so one man sharpens another." When we sharpen one another, that's tension, but such tension can be good. At each place God has called me to serve, someone has been present to sharpen me. People have sharpened my prayer life, my understanding of the Bible, and my love for people.

However, you cannot let tension work in your favor until you recognize how tension is working against you. Earlier I wrote of how insecure I was when I was younger. But in overcoming that insecurity, I overcompensated. I became arrogant. At the age of nineteen, when Jesus came into my life, I went from insecurity to cockiness. I was too self-assured.

When I started youth pastoring, I moved to a small town where a church of about one hundred people had seven youths in the youth ministry. After I spent a year ministering, it had four. I cried out to God one night in prayer. "Why, God, did you send me to these youth? Why has the youth ministry shrunk? Why did you do this to me?"

God spoke to my heart through his Holy Spirit, who seemed to be saying, *I don't trust you, Brian. You preach your word, not my Word.*

I was crushed. I had gone through Bible school, and I had been an intern. I was doing everything I had been taught. But, with a humbled heart, I tested the Holy Spirit's prompting with the reality around me. One woman in the church wouldn't send her three teenage kids to my youth group. I needed those kids; when you have only four kids, adding three can lift spirits immeasurably.

"Can I ask why you won't allow them to be involved in the youth ministry?" I asked her.

She didn't hesitate. "Because you don't preach the Word of God."

I could have done battle with her. To preserve my ego, I could have become my own public relations manager and defended myself. Though I'd strayed from the trajectory I should have been on, I did one thing right: I listened to the Holy Spirit.

"That's weird," I said to her, "because that's what the Holy Spirit told me a couple days ago."

Fortunately for me, this woman was an iron-sharpening-iron sort. Instead of allowing the tension of my failure to work against me and perhaps turn me from God, she encouraged me. She challenged me. She, in essence, said, "Let's find a way to use this tension to reconcile you and God and his purpose for you."

"Here's the deal," she said. "I'll send my kids to the youth group if you go with me to a weekend Precept Upon Precept workshop put on by Kay Arthur's ministry."

What did I have to lose? "Sure," I said.

It was amazing. In one weekend, I learned how to read the Bible and understand it for myself. This floored me. Then just as the woman at church had used tension to challenge me, I used tension to challenge my students.

I started preaching out of the book of Jude. We went from four kids to twenty. And it didn't stop there. Twenty became fifty, fifty became seventy-five, and seventy-five became one hundred. And remember where the problem started? In the tension of my own arrogance.

Tension as a Gift

When was the last time you thought of tension as a present for you to unwrap and use to make your life more than it's been? Until I began understanding the value of tension, I would have answered, "Never!"

Look at James 1:2–4: "Consider it a sheer gift, friends, when tests and challenges come at you from all sides. You know that under pressure, your faith-life is forced into the open and shows its true colors. So don't try to get out of anything prematurely. Let it do its work so you become mature and well-developed, not deficient in any way" (Message).

Is that cool or what? After I got over my arrogance, I was able to let the challenges and the pressure—the tension— mold me into what God wanted me to be.

Look at verse 2 closely. "Consider it a sheer gift." "Consider" is a translation of the Greek word *hēgéomai*, which means "to lead, to go before, or to go first." In other words, let the gift lead; let the gift go first. What is the gift we are to let lead? What is the gift we are supposed to let go first? Being able to view tension (tests, challenges, trials) as a gift that brings pure joy.

But what, naturally, *wants* to lead? For me, it's my anger or my frustration, not God's joy. Most of the time I'm so concerned about being right, being justified, being validated, or being liked that I forget to experience joy. Instead of increasing in the joy of the Lord, I increase in the fear of others.

The verses go on to say that we will have tension, tests, trials, and challenges of many kinds from all sides. Pressure is going to come from the north, south, east, and west. From without and from within. Some have preached otherwise. Some have said that if you come to know Jesus, all tension or pressure will just go away. James suggests otherwise, all the while counseling joy rather than worry. You can have joy despite the pressure.

I can remember, as a child, watching *Mutual of Omaha's Wild Kingdom*—an old-school version of Animal Planet. I remember scenes of lions coming from all sides to attack the gazelles. The lions would circle their prey and drive the herd toward another lion. Then they would feast together. I don't think of being circled by lions as joyful.

Isn't that how siblings treat the weakest child in the family? Isn't that how bullies on the playground treat the kid who can't read the eye chart? Isn't that how adults feel at work when their boss and colleagues start encircling them as if after prey?

Joy during Times of Tension

The New International Version of the Bible translates James 1:2–4 like this:

> Consider it pure joy, my brothers and sisters, whenever you face trials of many kinds, because you know that the testing of your faith produces perseverance. Let perseverance finish its work so that you may be mature and complete, not lacking anything.

Note the word *because*. I'm glad the Bible has "becauses." This passage would be a hard pill to swallow if it only said,

"Be joyful during trials." Instead, the Bible says there's a blessing for being joyful: that joy helps us develop perseverance. This is the big-life equivalent of the cross-country runner who faces trial after trial of long runs, interval work, maybe even a few daily doubles. Pain? Yes. The result? Perseverance—the ability to endure, to stay on their feet and run despite the pain, despite the tension, and, in a sense, *because* of the tension.

James is clear. We are to be joyful in trials because as we persevere, we mature. We are made complete. We lack nothing. Perseverance means we have grit, moxie, stamina, persistence, backbone. Like a diamond, we have to be tested, challenged, put under pressure to become perfect and complete, lacking nothing.

That's the kind of person God desires to create through the tension of everyday life. But when we refuse to accept tension as a gift, when we consider it an affront to the perfect life we believe we deserve, then, as the Message says, our "faith-life is forced into the open and shows its true colors" (v. 3).

Believe me. This is a lesson God taught me when my wife, Tanya, and I welcomed the arrival of our beautiful daughter, Isabella.

4

Tension at Its Best—Jesus!

There is no improving the future without disturbing the present.

Catherine Booth

Isabella was born on October 17, 2001, in our home in Post Falls, Idaho. She was a lethargic, laid-back baby. The midwife gave her oxygen right away. As she grew, we realized she was not meeting the expected milestones. She was sitting up and eating Cheerios, but she wasn't attempting to crawl or walk. Something seemed wrong.

"Consider it all joy, my brethren, when you encounter various trials" (James 1:2).

At age two, Isabella started to lose abilities. She stopped feeding herself Cheerios. She stopped sitting up. Tanya and I knew something was wrong. The tension in our home ratcheted up. We had no insurance, but we had to take her to a doctor. To pay the bills, I got a second job as a waiter. The joy in my life leaked out of me like blood from a wound. Looking back, I call this my angry season.

Isabella started pulling out all her hair. Tanya found a website (www.rettsyndrome.org) that explained Isabella's challenges. We were convinced she had something called Rett syndrome, but the doctors would not genetically test her for it because it was such a rare disease; they were highly doubtful that she could have it. Finally, we convinced a geneticist to do the test. In 2003, we unequivocally found that Isabella's MEcP2 gene was corrupt. She was officially diagnosed with Rett syndrome.

"... knowing that the testing of your faith produces endurance" (James 1:3).

Isabella has never walked or talked. Today, at age seventeen, she has a trach and a gastrostomy tube (G-tube). She has twelve hours of nursing care in our home—every single day. At different times in her life, we have lived in a pediatric intensive care unit (PICU). She has almost drowned in her own saliva from not being able to swallow.

"And let endurance have its perfect result, so that you may be perfect and complete, lacking in nothing" (James 1:4).

Isabella's disability has been the test of my life. The level of tension it has brought into our lives has been huge. I can remember the first five years of praying for Isabella and asking God to heal her. I kept thinking about "a God who is able but won't." On 60 Minutes, I learned about a woman who was a meth addict and a prostitute. She had a daughter named Isabella who was healthy and whole. Jealousy and frustration overcame me. How could a woman who was a meth addict and a prostitute have a healthy child? Meanwhile, I was a virgin on my wedding day and had no addictions, and yet my wife and I had a sick child. How was that fair?

I remember being in the hospital one night with Isabella. When I walked out into the waiting room, there was a little girl twirling in her new dress—not sick at all. Again, the tension rose.

A woman at the gym was asking me about my kids. I was listing each one of them and explained I had a special-needs child. She remained inquisitive. She asked good questions. Then she said, "I can relate. I have a cat that is blind." She then proceeded to compare her blind cat to my daughter. Something inside me wanted to scream, to vent about what an insensitive comparison it was.

But I reminded myself that God is good. My wife and I know how sweet heaven will be when Isabella talks for the first time, walks for the first time. I believe God can heal her instantly here on earth. However, if he chooses to give us that gift later in life or in eternity, I'm fine with that too.

As a pastor, I was officiating the wedding of a couple who is very close to me. As I saw the bride come down the aisle, it hit me. I will never walk Isabella down the aisle on her wedding day. Tears welled up in my eyes. The couple and the guests probably thought I was simply emotional because the woman is a good friend. I held myself together as best I could.

After the wedding, I sat in my car complaining to God about how I'd never have the chance to walk my daughter down the aisle. But God impressed this message on my heart: *Brian, listen. Fathers on earth walk their daughters down to mere men. You will get to walk your daughter down the aisle to the King of Kings and Lord of Lords. You will get to see your daughter dance for the first time when you are in my presence. The first word from your daughter's lips will be "Jesus." Don't feel sorry for yourself. Feel sorry for the fathers of this earth who will not get to experience what you will get to experience.*

I started to gain an eternal perspective, a perspective of the temporal versus the eternal. I was reminded that the tension of earth will be the triumph of heaven.

Open one eye to the world, and you will find tension. Open both eyes to the world, and you will be depressed. Set your eyes on Jesus, and you will find hope.

Jesus's Sacrifice Represents Tension at Its Best

Jesus, though 100 percent innocent, was sacrificed for the 100 percent guilty. That is tension.

The Son of God died for our sin on a cross. Tension.

Jesus was buried. Tension.

Jesus was resurrected to conquer our sin. Tension.

Jesus appeared to more than five hundred people who thought he was dead. Tension.

The Gospels make clear that Jesus was a man born to die. Tension.

Through faith in the gospel, a person is saved. Tension.

The gospel will stretch us. The gospel may even strain us. But in the end, it will do for us what we cannot do for ourselves.

Says Romans 5:6–8, "You see, at just the right time, when we were still powerless, Christ died for the ungodly. Very rarely will anyone die for a righteous person, though for a good person someone might possibly dare to die. But God demonstrates his own love for us in this: While we were still sinners, Christ died for us" (NIV).

God's love creates tension, Christ dying creates more tension, and my sin creates even greater tension. "Since we have now been justified by his blood, how much more shall we be saved from God's wrath through him! For if, while we were God's enemies, we were reconciled to him through the death of his Son, how much more, having been reconciled, shall we be saved through his life! Not only is this so, but we also boast in God through our Lord Jesus Christ, through whom we have now received reconciliation" (Rom. 5:9–11 NIV).

Some might say there isn't any tension in these verses. I respectfully disagree. They're full of tension. Christ dying on the cross—and our either running from that salvation or running to it—is the ultimate tension.

A Healthy Response to Tension

What is the difference between an unhealthy response to tension and a healthy one? Someone who responds to tension in a healthy way has many telltale characteristics. They are someone who

respects differences
communicates clearly
asks good questions
is humble
is helpful
listens more than talks

is kind
harnesses the energy in a room
allows debate
provokes thinking

Are you that kind of person? Remember, tension can either pull you away from the things that matter or push you toward those things. If you respond in a healthy way to tension, you welcome conflict as a way of strengthening your walk with God, your relationships with others, and your perspective on who you are in relation to both.

But to find that healthy response, you must first find yourself. You must know who you are, your uniqueness, your story.

PART 2
STORY

5

Everyone Has a Story

You and I are characters in God's Story, handmade by him.
Every character serves a purpose.

Randy Alcorn

After boarding a plane in Charlotte, I slipped into my seat for the flight back home to Seattle, exhausted from training all day. I was a modern-day Neil Page (Steve Martin) from *Planes, Trains & Automobiles*, politely wanting nothing to do with the person next to me, just wanting to keep to myself, to relax, to no longer be in social worker, trainer, peacemaker, mediator mode.

"Hi, my name's Sue," said my seatmate, a perky woman probably in her late forties.

"Uh, Brian," I said, offering my name with great reluctance.

"And what do you do for a living, Brian?"

I was sitting next to the female equivalent of Del Griffith (John Candy), Page's foil in *Planes*. I didn't want to divulge anything else, but, hey, how can you be salt and light in the world if you clam up and keep to yourself?

"I'm, uh, a public speaker, trainer, and mediator," I said. "I work for an organization that helps companies and individuals in conflict. I'm just returning from a long day of doing just that—and anxious to get back to my wife and four kids in Spokane."

Her eyes widened. "This is great!"

Without hesitation, she started to tell me about how she was a single mom who had raised her daughter, Alyson, the best she knew how. Alyson had recently gotten married. Sue had now been invited by and was on her way to see Alyson and her new husband. Prior to the marriage, Sue and Alyson had been best friends. They'd done everything together. They'd traveled the world. When Alyson had gone off to college, they'd texted or talked on the phone every day.

Whether I wanted to or not, I had been dragged into her life adventure. Suddenly, Sue started choking up.

"Now that she's married, I'll leave a message, and I won't hear back from her for two or three days. I know our relationship will not be the same, and I don't expect it to be. I just thought it would have some semblance of how it used to be. And I guess I'm hurt, although Alyson doesn't even know that. It's not as if they've shut me out; after all, they've invited me to come see them. But what do I do when I see her? Do I tell her that I'm hurt? I know this is so silly. I'm an adult, and she's an adult. What do I do?"

So through all this, I'm thinking, *God has me interacting with this woman for a purpose*. I looked her in the eye and said four words that need to be spoken at the beginning of any quest for reconciliation: "Tell me your story."

"My story?"

"Yes, from the beginning. What's your story?"

So much for relaxing. For nearly three hours, from taxiing to takeoff to leveling off at thirty-five thousand feet, she fed out her life story like kite string. As she did, I became far better equipped to help her deal with her dilemma. Why? Because understanding one another's stories helps us understand other people's perspectives and our own perspective. And perspective helps us be more compassionate and merciful. Our perspectives are shaped by the context of our lives.

Life is like a book. When you meet someone, you never know which chapter of their life you have entered. But when you figure that out, you're better able to relate to them. For example, when Sue said that she and her daughter used to do everything together—they were best friends—that suggested to me that she likely had a problem with *idolatry*. Idolatry happens when we make something so important that it breaks our relationship with God and others. I surmised that she also had *unmet desires*, which suggested to me that she was likely divorced and had probably come out of a difficult relationship. When she said that her relationship with her daughter couldn't be the same, I knew she was dealing with *disappointment*. But now I was asking her to unpeel the onion, so to speak.

"Well, I was raised in the Midwest," she began. "My parents stayed together all their lives. They recently passed away. My childhood was perfect. I was a farm girl, and I loved to climb trees and run around the little family farm. I did very well in school, and my parents sacrificed to send me to college.

47

"That's where I met Bob. He was tall and handsome. I fell head over heels in love with him. We soon married, and I quickly got pregnant and eventually gave birth to Alyson. That's when the real trouble began. Bob started trying to control everything I did. He became very jealous of my time with Alyson. He started yelling about how I never spent time with him. If I was ten minutes late getting home from the store, he would interrogate me. We would go visit my parents, and he would be very sweet and nice. Then we would get in the car, and he would spew the worst allegations at me, like that I was having sex with my dad. He was full of jealousy."

This was starting to sound like an *abusive relationship*. Sure enough: "One night he got so angry at me that he hit Alyson across the face, then came at me with a knife. I got Alyson and myself out of there for the night. We walked around a public park all night. She cried, and I would nurse her back to sleep. That's when I knew I had to get out. I planned for two weeks how to escape. I was so embarrassed. We had been married only two years, and I didn't want a divorce. I knew my parents wouldn't be happy. After two weeks, I checked myself into a domestic violence shelter. He tried to find me; they hid me from him. Eventually, I divorced Bob and moved to the East Coast. I was in my senior year of college. I graduated and then focused on raising Alyson and becoming a social worker. I was determined to help others."

"So Alyson grows up and—"

"Just like me, she gets married quickly."

I know where this is going, I said to myself.

She continued, "I was already very protective of Alyson and wanted the best for her. I'm just sad that our relationship has changed. I knew it would. I just didn't think it would be so quick."

There's power and clarity in people's stories, and if we'll just listen to those stories—and to our own—we'll be better equipped to find what most of us are ultimately seeking: reconciliation, peace, contentment.

"Sue, do you mind if I introduce you to a path that has always helped me? There are four steps: story, ascend, reflect, connect."

She was intrigued. "Interesting. Do explain."

I grabbed my drink napkin and drew a circle.

"You told me your *story*—the circle. Now let's *ascend*."

I drew an arrow up, within the circle, as if to God on high. "What core values do you have? What beliefs do you have about God that would comfort and guide you?"

"Well," she said, "I'm a Christian. I believe in the Bible. I believe God is with me."

"Do you believe you can pray to him?" I asked.

"Of course."

"Well, then, let's pray."

We prayed and asked God to give us wisdom and to comfort us. In other words, we ascended to God. We reached up to him for his strength, power, and wisdom—for his help. This in itself offers people a certain comfort; they're reminded they aren't alone in whatever difficulty they're facing.

"OK, so you've ascended. Now, let's *reflect*."

I drew an arrow pointing down, still within the circle of her story. "What fear is driving you, Sue?"

She paused a moment to connect some dots. I sensed this wasn't a level she'd been to before. "Well, I guess I worry that Alyson is experiencing the same thing I experienced."

"That's natural, but just because abuse happened to you doesn't mean it will happen to her. Sue, what do you *know* to be true about Alyson?"

"I know she's happy and busy balancing school and marriage. I know she loves me, and I know she loves her husband."

OK, so maybe the sky wasn't really as dark as Sue thought it was. She continued, "Alyson's husband has been very kind to me. He even sent me flowers on Mother's Day. His mom died when he was young."

"Many mothers-in-law don't get that kind of treatment," I said. "In his eyes, you obviously rock. And so does your daughter. He respects both of you."

A slight sense of pride touched her disposition, as if she hadn't realized that until now.

"So how do you want to *connect* with Alyson?"

I drew a horizontal arrow starting within the circle and going out of the circle to represent her story connecting with someone else's.

"I just want to have a good time with her and her husband. I don't want to have drama or stress. I'll be staying in a hotel because they have a small apartment. I just want to have a good time—all of us."

"That seems reasonable, and I don't see anything precluding that from happening, do you?"

"Well, I guess not."

"But here's the thing," I said. "You have the strength of the Lord within you, but it does no good if you don't rely on it. How about you start each day asking God to help you with your hurt and to give you a great time with your daughter and new son-in-law?"

For the first time since we'd been wheels up, she smiled. She looked as if a weight had been lifted from her shoulders.

"That sounds good," she said, "really good. I feel calmer already. I was thinking I was going to try to fix something, but now that I have some perspective, I'm not worried like I was. I think I ought to just wait and see what God can do through me."

"Amen to that," I said.

The plane soon touched down. The time had flown by. And I was reminded that as much as we'd like to keep to

ourselves sometimes, helping someone work through conflict (and working through our own conflict) means getting
involved, engaging with someone else, even getting out of
our comfort zones. I'm glad I did so, and I believe Sue was
too.

6

Our Stories Are Made
of Many Strands

Every human being is under construction from conception to death.

Billy Graham

Everyone has a story. We saw in the last chapter how we can look at our stories and interpret them. Let's go a little deeper. We all have *context*—interrelated conditions in which someone or something exists—that makes us who we are. Our backgrounds. Our experiences. Our parents. Our beliefs. Our geographic locations. The list of factors that shape us into who we are is endless. In other words, nobody lives in a bubble. We are who we are based on myriad factors—and the better we understand what those factors are, the better equipped we will be to deal with conflict. Furthermore, the better we understand the person or people we're in conflict with, the better equipped we will be to deal with conflict. In this chapter, we will see how context makes a big difference in our stories.

A friend of mine who's a journalist told me how someone wrote him a smarmy email about something my friend had written. Rather than let it go, my friend uncharacteristically lashed back at the man in an email. In return, the man shared a bit about his life, a sad life, really. Poverty. Insecurity. Loneliness. The more my friend read, the more he regretted having returned "evil for evil" (Rom. 12:17).

"Had I taken the time to learn the man's story instead of simply unleashing my venom on him, I wouldn't have made a bad relationship worse. I'd have been wiser to invite him out to lunch and try to build a bridge rather than create a wall."

Context matters. One of the reasons we experience tension is because of the context of our lives.

Now that we have the wide-angle view of context, let's take a close-up lens to it. What, specifically, are the elements that make us who we are? Our contexts are made up of a wide array of influences. I've divided these into ten factors.

Factor 1: Your View of God, Your View of God's Word, and Your Eternal Perspective

Whether you believe in God or not, your story contains an element of God. You may have dismissed him early in life. You may have said you don't believe in him. However, every human wrestles at some point with the God question.

Your view of God is extremely important because it shapes your story. If you feel God has let you down, your story is shaped or reshaped. If you feel like God exists but isn't present in your life, your story is shaped or reshaped. If you believe God is your Creator, if you believe God is your Judge, if you believe God is your Savior, your story is shaped or reshaped. Let me share some elements of God that have shaped my view of who he is:

- God is the Creator, and God is my Creator (Ps. 139:13–14; Isa. 40:28).
- God is holy and the ultimate Judge (James 4:12; 1 Pet. 1:14–16).
- God sent his Son as the Savior of the world and as my Savior (Rom. 5:6–8).
- God is my Protector (2 Thess. 3:3).
- God is good (Ps. 107:1).
- God is merciful (Ps. 145:9).

Your view of God shapes your story, but so does your view of God's Word. Think about the Bible verses I just mentioned. If you don't believe the Bible is real, authoritative, and accurate, then those verses won't impact you very much, if at all. Here is what I believe about the Bible. These beliefs have shaped my story:

- The Bible is inspired.
- The Bible is infallible.
- The Bible is authoritative.
- The Bible is accurate.

Factor 2: Your Relationship or Lack of Relationship with Your Father and Mother, Your Childhood, and Your Teenage Years

One of the greatest factors that shapes your story is your relationship to your earthly father and mother, biological or otherwise. I have both a biological father and mother and a stepfather and stepmother. I would never downplay the role my stepparents played in parenting me. They were both amazing, even though they were not my biological parents. All four of my parents shaped my story.

Some of you have never met your biological parents, maybe because you were adopted or because of tragedy and evil in the world. Parents who are killed by accidents or are victims of wars or terrorism leave so many orphans. The absence of those parents plays a huge role in shaping their children's stories.

Some kids are raised by abusive parents. The abuse can be physical, sexual, emotional, or maybe all three. The abuse can be neglect. Whatever the case, these situations shape their stories.

All kids are shaped by traumatic and mundane events that take place in their childhood or teen years. Being teased at school. Discovering you aren't athletic. Having a friend betray you. Having a girlfriend or boyfriend break your heart, or maybe breaking their heart. Being part of a family that moves a lot. Being raised in a family in the same town and the same house your entire life. All these events play a part in who you are now as an adult.

If you had great parents, an easy childhood, and fun teenage years, these things shaped your story. You may not be used to dealing with tension. You may have never seen your parents fight. You may not have dealt with rejection. Though nobody gets through childhood unscathed, success may come easily to you.

Whatever the case, your story is shaped by your upbringing.

Factor 3: Singleness, Marriage, and Other Intimate Relationships

Some people remain single all their lives. The freedom they have to do what God calls them to do is different from what someone who is married experiences. Obviously, if you are single, this is a huge part of your story.

If you are married, marriage shapes your story. So does the type of marriage you have. If you have a marriage that recovers quickly from setbacks, your life will be different from that of someone in a marriage in which one setback begets another and another. If you've experienced divorce, adultery, or the death of a spouse, it has affected your story like a tsunami affects people who live along a shoreline.

Intimate relationships outside of marriage also shape your story. Maybe you were promiscuous and now are living with the guilt and shame. Maybe you have forgiven yourself, but your spouse hasn't forgiven you. Maybe your spouse feels you continually compare them to others. Maybe you fear that people you had previous intimate relationships with will reappear in your marriage.

All intimate relationships influence and affect your story. All intimate relationships outside of marriage are sinful and affect your marriage. Yes, God forgives and restores, but that doesn't erase the intimate relationships from your story.

Factor 4: Having or Not Having Children

Choosing either to have children or not to have children can turn your story from *A Walk to Remember* into *Cheaper by the Dozen*. If you choose to have, adopt, or foster children, they will shape your story.

My kids have taught me so much about life, selflessness, humanity, and myself. They have taught me the basics of fun, the foundation of the gospel, and what it really means to be a loving father. Sometimes kids are like a mirror. Some attributes I like and other attributes I do not like. So I'm going to be different from someone who doesn't have children and learns their lessons in other ways. Neither scenario is better. They are just different.

Children, of course, come with no guarantee. Some people have children but have no relationship with their children. Parents who have been abandoned by their children have a story. Parents who have a great relationship with their children have a different story. In different ways, children shape your story.

Factor 5: Your Church Experience, Your Education, and Your Occupation(s)

You may not have been raised going to church. You may have been raised going to church all the time, whether you wanted to or not! You may have started attending as an adult. Your experience with church influences who you are. How often did you go? What type of church did you attend? Was it a high-liturgical church or a high-creativity church? You may have attended a denominational church, a nondenominational church, or an independent church. It may have been filled with older people, younger people, or a mix of generations. The church may have been multicultural or predominantly a single culture. All of this shapes your story.

And what your church taught you might be more significant than all the other factors put together. Were the priorities legalism ("Good Christians don't drink, dance, or chew—or go out with girls who do"), rules, dos and don'ts, and judgment? Or were grace, Jesus, the cross, the gospel, forgiveness, and freedom stressed? Did you laugh a lot? Or never laugh? Did the preaching emphasize topical teaching, exegetical teaching, or another kind of teaching? Was your worship subdued, or did you get physically involved with hand waving, foot stomping, and "praise the Lords"? Electric guitars or century-old organ? Communion? Baptism? All these factors affect your story.

If you went to church while you were growing up, you probably did so once or twice a week. But you more than likely attended school five times a week for nine months. That's a lot of influence from outside forces to change or reinforce who you are.

Whether in primary school, secondary school, middle school, high school, and/or college, teachers and your overall educational experience shaped you. You may have had a coach, band director, drama director, math teacher, science teacher, language teacher, or administrator who invested deeply in you. Your school experience may have been great or rotten. It may have been a launching pad to wondrous dreams or a prison cell you couldn't wait to bust out of.

And then, of course, there are the jobs you held and the job you currently hold, assuming you're employed. Your occupation has a huge effect on you. Some people are satisfied with their work life, while others are continually disappointed. Again, these are all strands of your story.

Factor 6: Your Friendships and Your Hobbies

Past friendships and current friendships influence your story. Your friends may inspire you to be better—to live better and to be all God created you to be. Or your friends—or perhaps "friends"—may pull you down, lead you astray, and bring out the worst in you.

Your hobbies and interests are also part of your story. Some people's hobbies are the focal point of their lives. They are ways to connect with friends and maybe even with their spouse. Others watch TV. Then there are video and computer games, in many ways an out-of-control hobby set. The person you are is influenced by whether you spend your weekends traipsing around the great outdoors or doing crossword puzzles.

Factor 7: Your Interpretation of Success and Failure

Your successes shape your story, as do your failures. Think about the tension success can bring. Think about the tension failure brings. You may have suddenly moved from success to failure. You may have suddenly moved from failure to success. Such shifts can't help but change you, mold you, inspire or depress you.

And how you interpret that success and failure plays a huge role in your story. If you see success as all-important and failure as the end of the world, you're going to be one kind of person. If you keep success in perspective and see failure as something that motivates you, you're going to be another kind of person. If you see yourself as mainly responsible for your success or failure, you're going to react one way. If, on the other hand, you trust God during failure and thank him for your success, you're going to react another way.

Romans 12:3 says, "For through the grace given to me I say to everyone among you not to think more highly of himself than he ought to think; but to think so as to have sound judgment, as God has allotted to each a measure of faith."

Factor 8: How You Process Bitterness and Forgiveness

Ephesians 4:31–32 counsels, "Let all bitterness and wrath and anger and clamor and slander be put away from you, along with all malice. Be kind to one another, tender-hearted, forgiving each other, just as God in Christ also has forgiven you."

Some people carry bitterness, anger, wrath, and slander everywhere they go. Their stories are shaped and reshaped by them. The lens through which they view life is blurred by their past hurts. They want to get even and talk negatively about those who have hurt them. Other people do not have this kind of lens on their vision. Which person are you? Bitterness has a huge influence on who you are and how you'll deal with conflict when it comes your way. And, of course, conflict will come.

Some people forgive fast and move on; they focus on the main things in life and let go of offenses. Others are quick to anger and slow to forgive. They hold on to hurts for months, years, sometimes decades. Even if they were unduly wronged, they are the ones who pay the price for the inability to let go. Your willingness or unwillingness to forgive also shapes your story.

Factor 9: How You Process Injustice and Justice

At some level, we all experience injustice in life. Maybe you were yelled at by a parent when you were innocent. Maybe you were disciplined by a teacher when someone else was in the wrong. Maybe you were taken advantage of by someone in authority. Maybe you were abused by someone more powerful. How much injustice you experienced—and how you processed or experienced it—shapes how you look at the world. Or perhaps you haven't experienced much injustice in your life. Then your story has been shaped accordingly.

A large part of today's racial divide in America exists because of the chasm between people who, as a group, know nothing about what it's like to be discriminated against and people who routinely experience discrimination. A big part of narrowing that gap is for those who haven't experienced discrimination to realize that others' experience has been different. In other words, learning someone else's story and contrasting it with your own pay huge dividends in resolving conflict. Such actions help you empathize with people whose experiences have been different.

Factor 10: Your Mindset

One of the most powerful shapers of your story is where you set your mind. Here are a few Bible verses about your mind.

Colossians 3:2 says, "Set your mind on the things above, not on the things that are on earth." Romans 12:2 says, "And do not be conformed to this world, but be transformed by the renewing of your mind, so that you may prove what the will of God is, that which is good and acceptable and perfect." And Philippians 4:8 says, "Finally, brethren, whatever is true, whatever is honorable, whatever is right, whatever is pure, whatever is lovely, whatever is of good repute, if there is any excellence and if anything worthy of praise, dwell on these things."

If you are continually setting your mind on earthly things, if you are continually conforming your mind to this world, if you are continually thinking of dishonorable things, they will influence your story.

I tell my kids all the time, "You need to tell yourself a different story. You need to tell yourself a God story." For instance, if my kids say, "Nobody likes me," I'll say, "You need to tell yourself a different story. God doesn't just like you; he loves you. Mom and I don't just like you; we love you." The stories you let play in your mind shape the story of your life. I'm not talking about positive thinking; I'm talking about *godly* thinking.

That's our next step in this journey: learning God's story so we can be less like us and more like him. But before we move on, I hope you understand how important it is to see yourself as part of your story and to see others as part of their stories. Doing so is absolutely critical in our quest to find common ground, quell disputes, and live at peace with one another.

7

Perspective Is Key
to Your Story

Life is 10% what happens to you and 90% how you react to it.

Charles Swindoll

I f you're serious about finding resolution, you must grasp how crucial it is to know yourself and the person with whom you're in conflict. Perspective is key to knowing both yourself and the other person, which leads to understanding your conflict and tension.

Using the ten factors outlined in the previous chapter, let's apply that kind of thinking to two stories involving tension, conflict, and stress: one a modern-day, true story of a couple I worked with and one a parable of Jesus involving a father and a wayward son. I will intersperse play-by-play commentary and analysis involving some of the factors to help you understand how our pasts are inextricably connected to the present, particularly when it comes to conflict. To help you follow my references to the factors that influence who we are and how we respond to conflict, here is the list of factors in a simplified form:

Factor 1: view of God

Factor 2: relationship with parents, childhood, and teenage years

Factor 3: singleness, marriage, and other intimate relationships

Factor 4: having or not having children

Factor 5: church experience, education, and occupation(s)

Factor 6: friendships and hobbies

Factor 7: interpretation of success and failure

Factor 8: processing of bitterness and forgiveness

Factor 9: processing of injustice and justice

Factor 10: mindset

Rick and Judy

Rick and Judy, when they first shared their story with me, were in their late forties and had been married for fourteen years. They had two boys, Cameron (twelve) and Nathan (ten). The couple ran a marketing company together, and conflict was their constant companion.

We began our conversation with prayer. "Now," I said, "tell me your story."

JUDY. I was raised in a Christian home [factor 1]. My mom and dad were very active in raising us [factor 2; this was significant because one of her complaints, I would later learn, was that her husband was *not* as involved in their children's lives as her father had been in her life]. We went to church every Sunday. I went to a Christian school [factors 1 and 5]. My brothers and sisters all graduated from the same Christian school in Texas. I was a cheerleader at school. I had a great childhood [factor 2].

BRIAN. Tell me a little more about your Christian home and your faith as a child.

JUDY. My family was filled with love. We went on mission trips together [factor 1]. We helped each other. Occasionally, my parents fought, but they would always make up and let us know that they had gotten things squared away [factor 2; this was significant because she was not experiencing this in her marriage]. Although I used to get annoyed by family devotions, we always had them. Does that help?

BRIAN. Yes, keep going.

JUDY. I went to college. My first degree was a bachelor of arts in marketing. I also got a master's in business [factor 5]. I always dreamed of having my own marketing firm, so after working in a firm for someone else for eight years, I talked to Rick about starting our own business [factor 5; this was significant because the business they started was in her area of expertise, not her husband's].

BRIAN. Is this before you got married or after [notice that
she brought up her business dream before she brought
up her marriage, which is suggestive of her priority]?

JUDY. Oh, yeah, Rick and I got married. I had already been
working for the marketing firm for about five years.

BRIAN. Tell me more about your marriage.

JUDY. I love Rick. He's very laid-back, but sometimes he
seems unmotivated, not interested, and distant [fac-
tor 2: opposite of her father]. Ever since we started
our own marketing firm, Rick and I have fought. I
get upset, and Rick doesn't say anything. He doesn't
seem to care [factor 7; she wants their marketing
firm to succeed, and Rick is less passionate about the
business than Judy is].

BRIAN. Judy, how would you describe the problem in
your marriage?

JUDY. I have to carry all the weight of everything. I have
to make sure the business succeeds. I have to make
sure the kids are taken care of. I have to make sure
the house is clean. I have to make sure everything is
done. So I'm frustrated all the time—on the verge
of wanting a divorce. If I have to do it all anyway, I
might as well do it on my own. At least I won't be
frustrated by Rick's lack of being a father.

BRIAN. OK, Rick, tell the story from your perspective.
And, please, don't try to rebut what Judy has said.
Just tell me your story.

RICK. I was raised in New York, mostly by my mom
[factor 2]. She was married three times. Her second
husband is my biological father [factor 2]. We never

went to church [factor 5]. I don't think I even believed there was a God [factor 1]. Maybe I did. When I was little, I can remember asking God if he was real and could he help my mom and me [factor 1]. Anyway, my childhood was not the most pleasant, but my mom tried her hardest. We moved a lot [factor 2]. My mom was a very hard worker. She had five kids, one from her first husband, two from her second husband, and two from her third husband. I was mostly raised by her third husband.

BRIAN. Tell me about your relationship with him.

RICK. He came into my life when I was seven or eight years old. He was good to me. He provided for us and really was into watching football, so we watched a lot of games together. Besides that, he mostly worked. He didn't ever go to my concerts at school or anything like that [factor 2; notice how his functional dad wasn't particularly involved]. That's why I don't get it when Judy says I'm not involved in the family. I go to all the boys' events. I go on bike rides with them. Sure, we have our down times, but I'm way more involved than my dad was [factor 4; note how he's grading on a curve, so to speak. Minimal involvement was par for the course for him as a kid, so doing *anything* seems like being involved to him. Judy, on the other hand, grew up with a totally involved father, so her definition of being involved is vastly different.].

BRIAN. How did you and Judy meet?

RICK. We met at church. I started going to church when I went to college. I met a student campus leader, and he invited me to go to his church [factor 5]. I didn't finish college. In the middle of community college, I stopped because I got a really good job at a utility company. It was an easy job and paid pretty well [factor 5]. I worked there for ten years before meeting Judy at church. So I had been going to church for ten years, and I was really enjoying life. I was in my midthirties. Judy had moved to town for her marketing firm, and she started attending the same church I did. I should add that before I started going to church, I had many girlfriends, and I was very sexually active [factor 3]. When I became a Christian, I had a lot of control until . . .

JUDY. He probably doesn't need to know that.

BRIAN. Rick, go ahead.

RICK. I had a lot of control after I became a Christian. But that changed when I met Judy. She was pregnant before we got married [factor 3], so we married very quickly. Two weeks after we got married, she miscarried [factor 9; they are dealing with loss]. Her parents were very angry because we got married so quickly. I really enjoyed working at the utility company, and Judy wanted to start this new company. I was all for it. Then it turned into, "Let's do it together." I wasn't all that excited, but I didn't want to tell her. She was so excited about it. She said she would teach me how to do it all. I thought maybe it is a good idea. I have been . . . I've been . . . Oh, never mind.

BRIAN. You've been *what*?

RICK. I've been regretting that decision ever since.

BRIAN. Why?

RICK. I go to work, and I can't do anything right [factor 7].
I went from having a wife to having a boss at work,
at home, at church, at everywhere. I'm so frustrated
[factor 9].

JUDY. That is not true.

BRIAN. Judy, let's not interrupt.

My time with Rick and Judy went on. However, I want
to pause here so you can see how the factors were playing
out in their lives. See "Factor Table for Rick and Judy"
for a summary with some additional details and some
observations.

Factor Table for Rick and Judy

FACTOR 1: VIEW OF GOD	
Judy	She was raised in a Christian home and has a long Christian history and tradition.
Rick	Christianity is fairly new to him; he has virtually no Christian history and tradition.
Observations	Judy compares her current family with her rich upbringing and feels something is missing. Rick compares his current family with the family he grew up in and doesn't sense anything is missing.

FACTOR 2: RELATIONSHIP WITH PARENTS, CHILDHOOD, AND TEENAGE YEARS	
Judy	She had a solid family and involved parents.
Rick	He had an involved mom, but he experienced hurt because of the absence of a father.

| Observations | Judy and Rick have far different expectations. Judy compares Rick to her dad and finds him lacking. Rick compares himself to his dad and stepfathers and finds himself more involved than they were. |

FACTOR 3: SINGLENESS, MARRIAGE, AND OTHER INTIMATE RELATIONSHIPS

Judy	Before meeting Rick, Judy was not sexually active. She is embarrassed about getting pregnant before she and Rick got married. Her parents don't know about the pregnancy. Hiding this bothers her.
Rick	Before meeting Judy, Rick was sexually active. He feels guilty because he pressured Judy into premarital sex. He felt pressured by Judy to marry her after she became pregnant.
Observations	Neither has sought or accepted God's grace and forgiveness in this area of their lives. As a result, they are each burdened by much hurt and frustration.

FACTOR 4: HAVING OR NOT HAVING CHILDREN

Judy	She believes she has an awesome relationship with her kids. She is busy. She knows they understand.
Rick	He believes he has an awesome relationship with the boys. He does a lot more than his dad or stepfathers did.
Observations	Judy and Rick reached their assessments of their efforts today by comparing themselves to past experiences. These perspectives are integral to their frustration.

FACTOR 5: CHURCH EXPERIENCE, EDUCATION, AND OCCUPATION(S)

Judy	She is living her occupational dream. Rick is the only drag on that dream.
Rick	He regrets quitting his utility company job. He feels as if he lost his wife and gained a full-time boss.
Observations	The work situation is where their two extremely different perspectives clash and friction is created.

FACTOR 6: FRIENDSHIPS AND HOBBIES

Judy	She didn't talk about friendships and hobbies.
Rick	He didn't talk about friendships and hobbies, though he mentioned going on bike rides with the kids.
Observations	This might seem insignificant but is actually a problem because Rick doesn't know how to make friends and how to keep friends.

FACTOR 7: INTERPRETATION OF SUCCESS AND FAILURE

Judy	She has had a lot of success in life. The only failure she has experienced has been in her relationship with Rick.
Rick	He has had a lot of failure and disappointment in life, which colors his view of life now. He felt most successful at his utility company job.
Observations	Judy's confidence clashes with Rick's lack of confidence. He feels inferior. She is impatient, thinking, "Why can't he be as good as me at work?"

FACTOR 8: PROCESSING OF BITTERNESS AND FORGIVENESS

Judy	She struggles with bitterness because of Rick's lack of involvement in the family and lack of energy at work.
Rick	He is bitter that he listened to Judy and quit a job he really enjoyed.
Observations	While bothered by Judy's control, Rick didn't express much frustration. Judy's frustration, meanwhile, was off the charts. Neither wants to forgive.

FACTOR 9: PROCESSING OF INJUSTICE AND JUSTICE

Judy	She wrestles with what she sees as an injustice from God regarding the miscarriage. She wonders if God was punishing her for having sex before marriage.
Rick	He isn't sure he would have married Judy had she not gotten pregnant.

Observations	Judy's sense of injustice and Rick's feelings of being in a marriage that he didn't really want to be a part of are big contributors to the chasm between them.

FACTOR 10: MINDSET

Judy	She is positive about herself, negative about Rick.
Rick	He is negative about himself, negative about Judy.
Observations	Judy is confident in herself. Rick lacks confidence and is just trying to get by.

During our meeting, Rick and Judy spent some serious time working through their problems. They decided Rick should seek a job that he was passionate about. They became more team oriented and less focused on "what's in it for me?" That, in turn, fueled the fires of encouragement. The result? A couple in conflict became a husband and wife who, although not perfect, were operating as God intended—with a new sense of oneness and God-centered purpose.

The Prodigal Son

What's the difference between our stories and Jesus's story? Our stories are forever flawed. His is the standard of perfection. His story is the story we aspire to make our own—one of living for others, loving unconditionally, and leaving behind the insignificant distractions of the world and concentrating on what really matters: our heavenly Father.

Jesus's one overriding story is a compilation of hundreds of Scripture-based stories, some of which he *lived* (making the blind man see) and some of which he *told* (the parable of the prodigal son). Let's delve into the latter because, though a centuries-old parable, it reveals the same things our modern-day conflicts are made of: tension, pride, ego, wrong thinking—the works.

A son demanded his inheritance, left home, squandered that inheritance, and stood on the threshold of despair. A father watched that son turn his back on him and go his own way. An older brother watched his selfish younger brother make a poor decision and seemingly get rewarded for it. Each, of course, saw a different story.

I'm not telling this story simply to teach the lesson of the prodigal son. Many of you already know that lesson. I'm offering this story to help us understand how different people can look at the same story in different ways. Let's begin with Luke 15:11–32.

> And [Jesus] said, "A man had two sons. The younger of them said to his father, 'Father, give me the share of the estate that falls to me.' So he divided his wealth between them. And not many days later, the younger son gathered everything together and went on a journey into a distant country, and there he squandered his estate with loose living. Now when he had spent everything, a severe famine occurred in that country, and he began to be impoverished. So he went and hired himself out to one of the citizens of that country, and he sent him into his fields to feed swine. And he would have gladly filled his stomach with the pods that the swine were eating, and no one was giving anything to him. But when he came to his senses, he said, 'How many of my father's hired men have more than enough bread, but I am dying here with hunger! I will get up and go to my father, and will say to him, "Father, I have sinned against heaven, and in your sight; I am no longer worthy to be called your son; make me as one of your hired

men.'" So he got up and came to his father. But while he was still a long way off, his father saw him and felt compassion for him, and ran and embraced him and kissed him. And the son said to him, 'Father, I have sinned against heaven and in your sight; I am no longer worthy to be called your son.' But the father said to his slaves, 'Quickly bring out the best robe and put it on him, and put a ring on his hand and sandals on his feet; and bring the fattened calf, kill it, and let us eat and celebrate; for this son of mine was dead and has come to life again; he was lost and has been found.' And they began to celebrate.

"Now his older son was in the field, and when he came and approached the house, he heard music and dancing. And he summoned one of the servants and began inquiring what these things could be. And he said to him, 'Your brother has come, and your father has killed the fattened calf because he has received him back safe and sound.' But he became angry and was not willing to go in; and his father came out and began pleading with him. But he answered and said to his father, 'Look! For so many years I have been serving you and I have never neglected a command of yours; and yet you have never given me a young goat, so that I might celebrate with my friends; but when this son of yours came, who has devoured your wealth with prostitutes, you killed the fattened calf for him.' And he said to him, 'Son, you have always been with me, and all that is mine is yours. But we had to celebrate and rejoice, for this brother of yours was dead and has begun to live, and was lost and has been found.'"

It's important to note that when *hearing* a story, we interpret it differently depending on our own stories. What's more, when we are *involved* in a story, we also interpret it differently depending on our own stories. So let's look, first, at the people Jesus was sharing this story with.

Luke 15:1 says, "Now all the tax collectors and the sinners were coming near Him to listen to Him." Jesus was teaching, and the nonreligious—the nonbelievers—were coming to hear him. Today, many of those listening to Christian messages are believers. But that wasn't the case in Jesus's day; many nonbelievers listened to him.

Luke 15:2 says, "Both the Pharisees and the scribes began to grumble, saying, 'This man receives sinners and eats with them.'" The Pharisees and the scribes were the religious people of Jesus's day. They were also listening to Jesus. When teaching this story, some pastors emphasize that sinners were listening. Others emphasize that religious people were listening. In fact, both were listening.

Why is this important? Jesus had a message for both the sinner and the religious person, even though each looked at the same incident with a different perspective. Likewise, when we're dealing with conflict today, each person involved in the conflict will look at the same incident with a different perspective. Jesus is saying, in essence, "There's a message here for you both."

In the case of the prodigal son, the sinner heard Jesus saying that the younger son wanted to do life his own way. He wanted his inheritance. He wanted to live sinfully. So the younger son went off and lived life as he wished. When things got tough, he wanted to fix his own problem. He went and hired himself out. His do-it-my-way pride was so strong that he resorted to feeding pigs rather than admit he was wrong and return home.

Then Jesus offered the key phrase, the catalyst that turned the young man's life around: "But when he came to his

senses . . ." On that fulcrum, the entire story pivoted. Everything changed. He went from darkness to light, hopeless to
hopeful, sinner to sinner saved by the grace of God.

Jesus was teaching the sinner that they had to wake up and
return to what they knew was right. The younger son began
to think about his father. He remembered how his father's
slaves were well taken care of, and yet he was starving. He
reflected on his sinfulness. And he began making plans to
reconnect with his father.

Remember the diagram in chapter 5? The first arrow of
the diagram is to ascend. Jesus was teaching that when your
story finds you at the end of you—and when you have come
to your senses—it's time to ascend, time to reconnect with
your heavenly Father, time to return to where you belong:
home and your heavenly Father.

Isn't that what all of humanity needs to discover? That
we are sinners, enemies of the cross, far from God? We have
broken our relationship with God by demanding to do life
our own way. Thus, each one of us must come to our senses.
We must ascend, realizing that God is good. Then we must
reflect by examining our stories so we can take responsibility. Then we must connect by going back to the heavenly
Father. When we approach him, we confess our sin to him.
We repent of our sin. We ask for mercy.

Ascend, reflect, and connect. Ascend by going back to the
heavenly Father. Reflect by taking personal responsibility.
Connect by confessing, repenting, and asking for mercy.

This is the relationship God wants with us. And guess what?
This is the same relationship he wants us to have with others.

If you have sinned against a friend, God wants you to
ascend—go back to your heavenly Father. God wants you to

reflect—take personal responsibility. And God wants you to connect—reestablish a healthy relationship with your friend. Rebuild bridges to those you've hurt, been hurt by, or both.

All of this is well and good, but let's not forget there's another side to this story beyond the sinner's perspective. The older brother was less than happy when his father embraced the wayward brother upon his return. Where was the justice in the father's actions?

When Jesus was telling the parable, the Pharisees and the scribes—the religious people—were not likely relating to the sinner. They were not empathizing with the once-was-lost-but-now-is-found son or the father who welcomed the young man home. After all, they didn't consider themselves sinners. They were righteous. So they related to the older brother. They saw the story through his eyes. They put themselves in his shoes. They were not celebrating. They were seething. They were not happy about the reconciliation. They were unhappy because they'd spent their entire lives considering themselves righteous and noble and right. But who was suddenly the star of the show? Their wayward brother.

What the older brother had in common with the prodigal son was this: both wanted to live their lives their own way. But only one—the prodigal—came to his senses and repented. The other—the older brother—had no interest in repentance, justice, and mercy. He wanted to live according to his own self-righteous works of the law. This was true for the religious people to whom Jesus was telling the story.

The sinner / prodigal son ascended back to the heavenly Father. The religious person / older brother refused to do so. One reconnected with God. The other had never really connected with God. The story ends with the older son wanting things his way instead of the father's way.

How does this relate to us? If we have a broken relationship with God or with our neighbor, God wants us to come to our senses. He desires that we run to him because he's running toward us. He desires that we reconnect with the two things that he says in Matthew 22:37–39 are more important than all else: God and others.

Doing this begins with understanding our stories and the stories of others. As we'll soon see, the more clearly we understand the stories, and the more clearly we find God's perspective, the more clearly we can find common ground, which marks the pathway to peace and reconciliation.

PART 3
ASCEND

8

Finding God's Perspective on Our Stories

Only looking through eternity can we have God's perspective.

Beth Backes

Two moms were talking at the park while their two sons played on the playground equipment.

MOM 1. How was your weekend?

MOM 2. Good, yours?

MOM 1. Horrible. I was driving when all of a sudden the car jerked to the right. I started hearing thump, thump, thump. I pulled over to find out I had a flat tire. I went to get the spare out of the trunk, and to my surprise, the tire wasn't there.

MOM 2. Wow. That *is* horrible.

MOM 1. That's not all. My phone battery died. So I had to wave my arms up and down to get someone to pull over to help. I was so humiliated.

MOM 2. Did anyone stop?

MOM 1. Yes, a state patrolman stopped. He turned on his lights. That was embarrassing. He didn't have an extra tire, so he called a tow truck.

MOM 2. I am so sorry.

MOM 1. We rode in the tow truck to the tire place. The tow truck drove so slowly it took forever. I think the tire repair place took me for all I was worth. It was a horrible day. Worst day ever.

Meanwhile, as they played nearby, the women's sons were also talking.

BOY 1. How was your weekend?

BOY 2. Good. Yours?

BOY 1. It was amazing! We were headed to buy school clothes when all of a sudden my mom started driving crazy. The car started going all over the road. It was awesome, like a chase scene in a movie! My mom pulled over. I guess she was driving so crazy because we blew a tire.

BOY 2. Cool!

BOY 1. That's not all. We got to wave our arms all around and jump around next to the highway. A police car came and its lights turned on. Blue. Red. Everyone was staring at us. I felt like I was on *Dancing with the Stars*—only without the dancing. The officer let me sit in the car. I saw his gun and all the buttons on his dashboard!

BOY 2. You're so lucky!

BOY 1. That's still not all. A big truck came. The guy used this big thing to get our car onto the back of his truck. Then I got to ride in the biggest truck I have ever ridden in.

BOY 2. Cool! Did he go fast?

BOY 1. No, but he took us to this place to fix our car. There was free popcorn. All you could eat. I gorged myself. I got to play in all the tires. I hid from my mom. It was awesome! On the way out, the man behind the counter gave me a candy. It was a blast! Best day ever!

What Is Perspective?

We want to get beyond our own perspective and the other person's perspective to God's perspective. To do this we must notice that facts are different from perspective. Facts are the observable parts of a situation that any two people can see. Perspective is based on the interpretation of those facts. In the flat tire incident, two perspectives were at play, and the only shared points were the basics of the incident, those observable occurrences both parties agreed on. The two were in a car. The car had a flat tire. A police officer got involved. A tow truck took mom, son, and car to a tire repair shop. Beyond that, what the mother saw as the worst day ever, her son saw as the best day ever.

Do you see how important it is to understand both your story and other people's stories? If you assume that other people look at the world just as you do, your chances of overcoming conflict with such people are slim. And your chances of being empathetic to their plights are slimmer. You end up with lose-lose instead of win-win outcomes. There are the facts, and there are the perspectives based on the interpretations of those facts.

Life is not a formula, but if it were, a perspective formula might look something like this:

> your story as filtered through your past experiences and core beliefs + your interpretation of the present situation in the context of your environment + healthy/unhealthy use of tension = your perspective

In this case, the mother's interpretation of the flat tire incident might have been clouded by her past. Maybe her parents were never there for her, so the incident conjured up anger because it was a reminder that she had been alone against the world. Maybe she was made fun of at school, so the flashing police lights and the ride in the tow truck brought back painful memories of being humiliated. Maybe her present situation includes a lack of time and money, so having to buy a new tire and wasting an afternoon waiting for a repair made her want to shake a fist at God.

And the little boy? Perhaps he was baggage-free at this point of his young life, so he could interpret the event as simply a fun afternoon. Here's the difference between the mom and the little boy: the facts for each were exactly the same; the interpretation of those facts (perspective) made all the difference.

Now let's leave mother and son behind and broaden our perspectives. What perspectives do we have? What perspectives influence how we live? They depend on what drives us, right? If we think prestige gives life meaning, we live with the perspective that living in the right kind of home, driving the right kind of car, wearing the right kind of clothes are important. If we think power gives life meaning and we work so we can climb the ladder, we're less likely to care about whose hands we step on as we ascend that ladder, and we perhaps grow insecure when we feel we're losing power. If we think accomplishment gives life meaning, we achieve so we can feel good about our success. We set and accomplish goals so we can remind ourselves that we are significant. We are willing to sacrifice all sorts of things—relationships or even our connection with God—because we are driven to achieve.

These are a few examples of perspectives people might have. Now let's contrast them with God's perspective, because when facing a conflict, we want to ascend beyond our own perspective to God's perspective.

God's Perspective

First, God has a heart perspective. "But the LORD said to Samuel, 'Do not look at his appearance or at the height of his stature, because I have rejected him; for God sees not as man sees, for man looks at the outward appearance, but the LORD looks at the heart'" (1 Sam. 16:7).

This verse is about Samuel selecting a new king for Israel. The new king would eventually be David. Although this passage is about David, we learn something about God and how he interacts with humankind. He has a heart perspective. In other words, God evaluates all our internals because internals, not externals, are most important.

Part of me is excited that God looks at my heart and not my outward appearance. Another part of me is afraid because God looks at my heart and not my outward actions. Why the spectrum from excitement to fear? Fear because I know who I am. Excitement because I know who I am in Jesus.

In any given situation, God has a distinctly different perspective. He's looking at not only our outward actions but also our hearts. He's filtering every experience, every injustice, and every tension through his Son, Jesus.

Second, God weighs our motives to reveal our perspectives. "All the ways of a man are clean in his own sight, but the LORD weighs the motives" (Prov. 16:2).

This is part of a believer's story. The Holy Spirit takes each element of our stories and weighs not only the facts but also the motives behind those facts. We have all been in a conversation with someone we want to impress. We may exaggerate or even stretch the facts. God knows and weighs those motives.

Proverbs 16:2 is key to understanding perspective. Your perspective may seem right in your eyes, and my perspective may seem right in my eyes, but we need to ask the Lord to show us our motives.

Third, God searches our hearts and tests our minds so that we may see our perspectives. "The heart is more deceitful than all else and is desperately sick; who can understand it? I, the LORD, search the heart, I test the mind, even to give to each man according to his ways, according to the results of his deeds" (Jer. 17:9–10).

This Scripture passage points out that our hearts are deceitful. Like it or not, that's our default because of the sin nature with which we're born. The human side of us will typically think of our hearts as pure and the heart of the person we're in conflict with as deceitful, impure, or malicious. The reality is that our hearts and their heart are deceitful, impure, and malicious. The gracious position is to see the fallenness of our hearts and the redeemed nature of their heart.

God not only searches our hearts but also tests our minds. How God does this is beyond me. However, I do know that our thoughts before, during, and after tension are very important to God. One of the key elements of our minds is where we set (or focus) our thoughts. If we want to gain a true perspective on a situation, we must be willing to set our minds on the things above (ascend). To gain a clear human perspective, we must have a clear God perspective. Colossians 3:1–2 says, "Therefore if you have been raised up with Christ, keep seeking the things above, where Christ is, seated at the right hand of God. Set your mind on the things above, not on the things that are on earth."

We have to take control of where we set our minds. If our minds are fixed on God's perspective, we will pass the heart test. Here's a simple exercise to begin gaining God's perspective: write or say a prayer asking God to look inside you, weigh your motives, search your heart, and test your mind. This prayer may look something like this: "God, I'm experiencing tension. Some of the tension I'm experiencing may be leading to healthy responses and some may be leading to unhealthy ones. I need to gain perspective. Will you look inside me? Will you weigh my motives? Will you search my heart? Will you test my mind? I want to have your perspective, not mine, in this situation."

When conflict comes, it's easy to react based on our own perspectives rather than God's. But when we see with God's eyes, we can resolve conflict, we can learn lessons, and we can glorify God.

Having just completed a pastor training event at an out-of-town church, I was with my family at a steakhouse with friends when our two-year-old son, Isaiah, pulled two little plastic toys out of his pocket.

"Where did you get those?" I asked him.

"I bought them."

I knew that wasn't the case. "Isaiah, did they give those to you in the nursery?"

"No," he said. "I took them."

"Well, we have to take them back then," I said. "Those don't belong to you."

After our meal, we returned to the church. It was all locked up. Our hotel was a half hour drive in the other direction. The simple solution was just to forget about what he had done. But when I looked at things from God's perspective, the Holy Spirit seemed to be saying, *Return in the morning.* So we did, even though the church was in the opposite direction of home. I explained to the secretary what had happened and then had my son come in to apologize.

"I'm sorry I took the toys," my son told her. "Will you forgive me?"

"We forgive you," she said. "Thank you for having the courage to come back."

Isaiah started to cry, but as we left the church, he grabbed my hand. "Dad," he said, "I think God is happy with me now."

"I think you're right."

And then I started to cry.

In our relationships with others, we are challenged each and every day. Are we going to look at situations through selfish eyes or God's eyes? Are we going to wear blinders, or are we going to consider not only our stories but also the stories of others? In Rick and Judy's situation, the only way they could make their relationship healthy was to do the following:

understand how their own life experiences influenced them in certain ways

understand how their spouse's life experiences influenced him or her in certain ways

look at their relationship from God's perspective to find solutions that would be honoring to him

Having a God perspective requires us to do three things, none of which are easy but all of which have the power and the potential to resolve conflicts and to reshape our relationships into ones of peace, not contentiousness.

Approach the conflict with a heart perspective. Resolving a conflict is not about us winning and the other person losing. It's not about us looking good. It's about making things right on a heart level.

Understand our motives. If we've managed to approach the conflict with a heart perspective, then we're willing to examine our motives as objectively as possible. Maybe those motives are pure; most likely, they're tainted with a subtle desire to get our way, perhaps even to make the other person pay a price for treating us poorly.

Search our hearts for any malice, any desire to get even, or any blindness that might be preventing us from seeing a bigger picture.

When it comes to conflict, the alternative, frankly, is what most people choose. They don't dare approach a conflict with a heart perspective because, deep down, they don't want to face their own fallenness. They don't dare examine their motives because, deep down, they don't want to face their own selfishness. They don't dare search their hearts because, deep down, they don't want to see the bigger picture. You see, discovering our sinfulness—let's just call it what it is— results in the feeling that we have an obligation to change. And change can be hard, so we avoid it.

Instead, most people simply fight. They control. They push their point of view on the other person. They try desperately to win the argument, to prove the other person wrong, to make themselves look good and the other person look bad. As we continue our journey into finding peace in the midst of conflict, I ask only one question: How's that working out? If the answer is, as I suspect, "Not so well," perhaps it's time to do something to create a new story. It's never too late to write a new chapter in your life.

9

Recognizing God's Presence

The voice you believe will determine the future you experience.

Steven Furtick

A friend of mine is attempting to hike the entire 2,650-mile Pacific Crest Trail, which stretches from Mexico to Canada. Each summer he tackles 200 to 500 miles of the trail. I asked him how he went from being an inexperienced hiker to being able to hike twenty to twenty-five miles per day. He mentioned vigorous training. He mentioned planning. He mentioned getting the proper equipment.

"But the most important thing," he told me, "was studying the masters. The masters are the sage hikers who've been on every inch of the trail in every type of condition and have shown themselves worthy of being listened to. They know what I don't: how to cross the rivers when the snowmelt is heavy, how to avoid slipping on a snowy mountainside, how to keep going even when your body says no. And so I listen to them. I learn from them."

The same advice holds for those seeking to navigate the treacherous trails of conflict in an attempt to reach healthy relationships at home, at work, at church, or wherever they go. Nothing is more important than listening to the Master, the One who has gone before and knows how to get through all the dangers along the way.

We've talked about how life is full of tension, with some tension working for us and some working against us depending on our response (part 1). We've talked about how each of us has a story and that the better we know our stories and the stories of those around us, the better equipped we are to reach peaceful resolutions in times of conflict (part 2). But being aware of what we're facing and being well-equipped to face it isn't enough. Not by a long shot. We need someone—or rather Someone—to look to who can offer the direction, wisdom, strength, and grace we can't attain on our own.

We need God, plain and simple.

Five critical elements are involved in reconciling every relationship. But this is a battery-required process, and the battery that drives each one—the power to turn war into peace—is God. If he's not involved in the process, the process is doomed to fail.

So what are these elements for relationship reconciliation?

Element 1: recognizing God's presence
Element 2: understanding God's character
Element 3: understanding our identity in Christ

Element 4: living with an eternal perspective

Element 5: embracing our calling to be peacemakers

"But wait a minute," some of you may be saying, "I thought this was a book about overcoming conflict to create healthy relationships." You want to cut to the how-to part, to the secret-ingredients part, to the chase.

First, if that's you, I love your passion for wanting solutions. So do I!

Second, resolving conflict takes time, patience, and foundation building.

And, finally, understanding who God is and who you are in him is the secret ingredient. It's the how-to part. It is, in essence, the chase.

In the old days, when a bucket brigade went to work to put out a fire, part of its success was due to sweat equity and a cooperative system, two ingredients that come into play when overcoming conflict. But you know what actually puts a fire out. Water. In our case, the living water Jesus talks about in John 4:14: "But whoever drinks of the water that I will give him shall never thirst." To attempt to quell a conflict and bring about reconciliation without understanding who God is and who we are in him is to attempt to put out a fire without water.

So in part 3, let's build that foundation, starting with recognizing God's presence during conflict and reconciliation.

God's Presence during Conflict

Do you believe God goes before you? And how does that belief align with your attitude, prayers, and peace in the midst

95

of conflict? Do you believe God is present in the middle of your tension? Do you believe God goes before you even when you are experiencing trials in your life?

Here's what I find in my life: in the great times, in the happy times, in the times of success, I experience God's presence. When I prepare a sermon, I experience God's presence. When I'm in the Word, when I'm deep into devotions, I experience the presence of God. You're probably the same way, right? When your spiritual ship has come in and you're safe from sin, it's easy to feel God's presence.

But how about in the midst of tension? When you lose your cool? When the one you promised to love and honor has betrayed you? In short, when things get messy. Do you sense God's presence then? I hope so, because as you'll see, that's when we need his presence most. In the midst of the conflict.

Let's look at God's presence with people throughout history, understanding that God doesn't stop being God when the Bible is closed. He's with us. Here. Now. Today. Still, we can learn lessons from the past that will help us overcome conflict today, the foremost of which is the realization that God is with us.

Abraham and God

God interacted with Abraham a number of times. In Genesis 15:1, God says, "Do not fear, Abram, I am a shield to you; your reward shall be very great." A shield protects. A shield is held near to the body. In other words, God is close. God is near. Abraham believed God; God credited him as being righteous.

How can the story of Abram, renamed Abraham, help us? By understanding that whatever the tension we face, God is with us. He's our shield. We can go into his presence. He can transform us. He desires to change our old way of living into a new way of living.

Moses and God

God interacted with Moses, Moses sought his favor. In Exodus 33:14, God says, "My presence shall go with you, and I will give you rest."

God didn't say, "Good luck." God didn't say, "I'll send you out alone." God said, "I will go with you. My presence will go with you." God promised not only to go with Moses but also to give Moses rest.

"If Your presence does not go with us, do not lead us up from here," said Moses (Exod. 33:15). I love this about Moses. He said, in essence, "If you don't go with me, God, then I don't want to go." We need to have the same attitude Moses had, particularly when facing a conflict: "God, if your presence will not go with us into this conflict, we don't want to go."

Jonah and God

Abraham and Moses embraced the presence of God, but Jonah fled from it. God told Jonah to go to Nineveh because Nineveh's wickedness had become great. In Jonah 1:3, we read, "But Jonah rose up to flee to Tarshish from the presence of the LORD. So he went down to Joppa, found a ship which was going to Tarshish, paid the fare and went down into it to go with them to Tarshish from the presence of the LORD."

Though called by God to lead a people, Jonah fled. Then he was swallowed by a whale, lived in the belly of the whale for three days, was spit out, preached to the people of Nineveh, and they came to know God.

In the midst of tension, we can be like Jonah. We can try to flee the presence of God. But, fortunately, God is greater than our disobedience. He will do whatever it takes to get us back on track, even if that means sending a gigantic fish to swallow us up. Don't get me wrong; we have some responsibility in our relationship with God, but God has sovereign control. God is greater. God is more powerful. Which is why we should *want* his presence with us.

Jesus Invites Us into His Presence

Jesus says, "Come to me, all you who are weary and burdened, and I will give you rest. Take my yoke upon you and learn from me, for I am gentle and humble in heart, and you will find rest for your souls. For my yoke is easy and my burden is light" (Matt. 11:28–30 NIV).

No matter what you are going through, go to Jesus. If you and your wife are fighting, go to Jesus. If you're fighting with a coworker, go to Jesus. If you're leading and people are not following, go to Jesus. He is the source of life. He is the source of rest. He is the source of all comfort. I'm convinced that the major cause of burnout is our decision not to seek that comfort.

"Come to Me"

How do we go to Jesus? We go to him in faith. Faith is interesting. Christians believe they are saved by faith; however, many operate as if works will keep them safe. Works do not keep us safe. Faith in Christ saves us, and faith keeps us. In the midst of trials, conflicts, or tension, we often do not live by faith. We begin our relationship with Christ by faith, and then we try to figure out everything else in life by works.

Hebrews 11:1 says, "Now faith is confidence in what we hope for and assurance about what we do not see" (NIV). Be confident, have hope, walk in assurance even when you do not see how the things we are hoping for will come about. Not everything can be seen. Some think if they ascend to God, all their problems will instantly be fixed. No. This is not necessarily the case. But at the very least, you will not be alone as you seek to better your situation.

"All You Who Are Weary"

In life, we get worn-out. We get beaten down. We feel as if we're going to faint. But what does Jesus say? Come to him, all you who are weary.

If you are weary in your marriage, Jesus is there for you.

If you are fatigued at work, Jesus is there for you.

If you are burned out in ministry, Jesus is there for you.

If you are torn down because of your kids, Jesus is there for you.

Through prayer, Jesus will refresh you. Through his Word, he will energize you. Through his presence, he will comfort you.

"All You Who Are . . . Burdened"

What does it mean to be "burdened"? The Greek word is *phortizō*, and it could be used to describe a ship that has been overloaded with freight. What happens to an overloaded ship? It sinks. In the middle of relational tension, the ship of your heart can feel overloaded. If you are overburdened, if your ship is overloaded, if your heart is heavy, turn to Jesus. He will take the load onto his shoulders and carry it for you. When the seas are high and the winds are strong, he will keep you afloat.

"I Will Give You Rest"

How much rest we experience depends on our view of God, our faith in God, and our trust in God. Why? Because he's already promised his side of the bargain: I will give you rest. Our responsibility is to accept that rest, and that involves willingly trusting him. People who are easily worked up do not receive God's rest. They run around and make a lot of noise, but they don't rest. Do you believe God is actively present in your conflicts? Then trust him to take the burden of those conflicts. And rest.

"Take My Yoke upon You"

Jesus's yoke is light. He wants you to know that although he asks something of you, what he asks results not in a burden but in a blessing. He will shoulder your burden. Matthew 11:30 says: "For My yoke is easy and My burden is light."

"And Learn from Me"

There is much we can learn from Jesus. Talk about tension, stress, and conflict. Herod tried to kill him as a baby. The Pharisees hated him. The Sadducees grumbled about him. All the people who should have rejoiced at his coming despised him. How did Jesus respond? He taught them—with truth, with stories, with love.

What can we learn from Jesus as we go through conflicts? Here are seven lessons we can learn from Jesus's experiences.

1. *Jesus met conflict with humility* (John 8:1–11). In John 8, Jesus comes to the aid of a woman about to be stoned. He was in a stressful situation, being tested. But instead of squishing his doubters like bugs, he stooped down and kindly but clearly said, "He who is without sin among you, let him be the first to throw a stone at her" (v. 7). Think about his position. He didn't stand on a rock to get higher than they were. He stooped down. He humbled himself. Then he challenged them.

Humility has the power to change everything. It is one of the most important lessons we can learn from Jesus. Jesus changed the world with humility.

2. *Jesus took time for everyone.* Jesus hung out with sinners, and Jesus hung out with saints. Jesus spent time with those who opposed him, and he spent time with those who appreciated him.

- Jesus spent time with sinners: Luke 15:1
- Jesus spent time with grumbly, religious people: Luke 15:2
- Jesus spent time with seeking, religious people: John 3:1–2
- Jesus spent time with rich sinners: Luke 19:1–3

Sometimes conflict comes because we're dealing with people who are quite different from us. Surprise! Jesus hung out with all sorts of people, many of whom flat out opposed him.

3. *Jesus had his eyes on the main thing* (Luke 19:10). When we are in a conflict, we need to keep our eyes on the main thing. I have a friend who always says, "Let the main thing be the main thing."

So what was Jesus's main thing?

Jesus's main thing was and is to find those who are living outside the gospel and to see them saved. In any conflict we are experiencing, that needs to be our main thing. People do not need our rightness. People need Jesus. People need to experience the gospel through the way we handle our differences.

4. *Jesus's heart and actions were to do the will of his Father* (John 4:34). If each of us focused on the Father's will instead of our own wills, our lives would change significantly. Doing the Father's will sustains us through conflict.

5. *Jesus prayed—a lot* (Luke 6:12). Jesus was in a constant conversation with his Father. He relied on those conversations. Oftentimes, when we are in the midst of a conflict, we go to everyone but God. We need to run to God. God isn't opposed to our getting wise counsel from others, but we should also request wise counsel from the King of Kings. God is and will always be the greatest solution to any conflict.

6. *Jesus stood his ground on the most important things* (Matt. 21:13). To link arms with Jesus is not to be a weakling. Sometimes we need to take a stand for what is right. Jesus was not afraid to confront those who turned God's house into a marketplace instead of a house of prayer.

Jesus stood for and still stands for what is right and what is righteous. Sometimes in our conflicts, we take a stand on the minor issues instead of the major issues. We need to remember that the most important thing is modeling and living out the gospel in front of others.

7. *Jesus forgave* (John 21:15–17). Jesus told one of his followers, Peter, that he would deny Jesus three times. Soon after, Peter did just that. What did Jesus do? He forgave Peter and sent him back out to do the work planned for him.

Forgiveness is probably one of the most difficult lessons to learn from Jesus, and forgiveness is especially difficult during conflict. But I will guarantee this result if we learn it: we will have a lighter yoke. A person who holds on to bitterness will be weighed down.

So if we're to ascend to God, if we're to approach conflict the way Jesus approached conflict, we need to follow Jesus's example:

- Meet conflict with humility.
- Take time for everyone.
- Focus on the main thing.
- Do the Father's will.
- Pray.
- Stand our ground on the important things.
- Forgive.

When God is present and working through us, these elements show through. These elements help us bring about reconciliation out of conflict. Why? Because they reflect the very character of God, which is our next stepping-stone in this journey to peace.

10

Understanding God's Character

The great thing to remember is that, though our feelings come and go, [God's] love for us does not.

C. S. Lewis

My wife and I had been debating an issue regarding our daughter's health care for years. There had been numerous arguments, and we changed directions a few times. It created a lot of conflict, both in me and between us. But then the Holy Spirit pointed out God's character as the great Physician and Protector to help direct me in my conflict with my wife. I needed to trust God to take care of our daughter (and all our kids) and to honor my wife by trusting her perspective.

When it comes to conflict, we must understand that any conflict is not only about us and the person we're in conflict with. It's about God, in particular, the unchanging character of the Father that Jesus modeled. When we muster the humility, the courage, and the smarts to let God lead, we greatly improve our chances of resolving conflict.

God's character is witnessed in and through the Father, the Son, and the Holy Spirit. Oftentimes, in the middle of a conflict, we fail to allow God's character to leaven our responses. Ephesians 5:1 says, "Therefore be imitators of God, as beloved children." First Peter 1:16 says, "You shall be holy, for I am holy." We need to let the character qualities we see in God, in Jesus his Son, and in the Holy Spirit comfort us and lead us to live in the same way.

So what is the "same way"? What is the character of God? We could write an entire book about his attributes, but here are a handful that often come into play when seeking to resolve conflict.

The Father is compassionate and gracious. "Then the LORD passed by in front of him and proclaimed, 'The LORD, the LORD God, compassionate and gracious, slow to anger, and abounding in lovingkindness and truth; who keeps lovingkindness for thousands, who forgives iniquity, transgression and sin; yet He will by no means leave the guilty unpunished, visiting the iniquity of fathers on the children and on the grandchildren to the third and fourth generation'" (Exod. 34:6–7). Compassion and grace may not be two attributes that quickly come to mind when we think of God, but that is who our heavenly Father is. God is sympathetic to the trials we are going through. God is concerned about our conflicts. He wants to show us grace—unmerited favor. We don't deserve it. We didn't earn it. We can't purchase it. We can't work our way to it. He simply lavishes his grace on us because he loves us unconditionally.

The heavenly Father is slow to anger, even if we've turned against him. He abounds in lovingkindness and truth. When I fight with my spouse, she doesn't experience much lovingkindness. God is different. We need more of him and less of us.

The Father is close to the brokenhearted. "The LORD is near to the brokenhearted and saves those who are crushed in spirit. Many are the afflictions of the righteous, but the LORD delivers him out of them all" (Ps. 34:18–19). When conflict strikes, God is near us. He will save us when conflict crushes our spirits. When we are crushed by the words and actions of others, God is near. When we are crushed by our own horrible words, actions, thoughts, desires, and behavior, God is near.

If you love Jesus, you will experience much affliction, but God will deliver you from it. Don't get down. Don't give up. Don't lose hope. Look up. You can make it through conflict because Jesus went through the greatest conflict of all—with sin and death. His character can become your character.

The Father is good. "For the LORD is good; His lovingkindness is everlasting and His faithfulness to all generations" (Ps. 100:5).

Have you determined that God is good? As I mentioned, I have a disabled daughter. She has Rett syndrome. She has never walked. She has never talked. She has a tracheotomy. She has a G-tube. I remember a time of prayer when it hit me: God is good.

So many times people try to figure out if God is good in the middle of their struggles. They go from circumstance to circumstance trying to decide whether he is. Then when their circumstances overwhelm them, they say, "God isn't good."

The truth is that God is good despite our circumstances. God is good because that is his nature. We must determine that, no matter what, God is good.

The Father hears our prayers.

> I love the LORD, because He hears
> My voice and my supplications.
> Because He has inclined His ear to me,
> Therefore I shall call upon Him as long as I live.
> The cords of death encompassed me
> And the terrors of Sheol came upon me;
> I found distress and sorrow.
> Then I called upon the name of the LORD:
> "O LORD, I beseech You, save my life!"
>
> Gracious is the LORD, and righteous;
> Yes, our God is compassionate.
> The LORD preserves the simple;
> I was brought low, and He saved me.
> Return to your rest, O my soul,
> For the LORD has dealt bountifully with you.
> (Ps. 116:1–7)

Have you ever felt like God doesn't hear you? There's nothing wrong with wondering if God hears you. However, always come back to the truth that God does hear you. Always come back to the truth that God does incline his ear to you.

Will you commit to call upon and talk to him as long as you live? If your conflicts are great, talk to God. If conflicts are brewing, talk to God. If your family dynamics are horrible, talk to God. He hears your prayers.

11

Understanding Who
We Are in Christ

What you believe about your identity in Jesus will ultimately determine what you do to glorify Jesus.

Pastor Tim Yetter

Pastor Jeremy came to me angry. He felt slighted by his church board. For eighteen years, he had led the church. He had poured out his blood, sweat, and tears. Now the elders were saying that he wasn't good enough, that he was not a good leader. He was beyond frustrated.

"I feel as if God has abandoned me," he said. As we talked, we found his wounds went even deeper, his thoughts about God even bleaker. He was questioning God's love for him. He was wondering if there even was a God.

"What do I tell my wife?" he asked. "What do I tell my four children?"

You name it, he felt it. Angry. Isolated. Afraid. "What did I do to deserve this?" he asked.

I hurt for Pastor Jeremy. Nobody likes to be told they aren't measuring up. But what was making the problem worse was lost perspective. He was confusing his identity as a pastor with his identity as a follower of Christ. He was allowing himself to be defined by those around him and not by God. He was having an identity crisis.

When we face a crisis, it reveals who or what we really trust. For example, some people put their ultimate trust in their work. But, as Pastor Timothy Keller said in an interview discussing his book *Every Good Endeavor*, "When you make your work your identity . . . if you're successful it destroys you because it goes to your head. If you're not successful it destroys you because it goes to your heart—it destroys your self-worth."[1]

Some people trust money. Some trust achievement. Some trust a political party. Anything we trust wholeheartedly in place of Christ becomes an idol that will ultimately turn on us, let us down, offer a false sense of security, particularly in times of crisis. Pastor Jeremy's identity was in his position; it had become so important to him that it clouded his perspective of who he was in Christ. His position, not Christ, was on the throne of his life.

Here's what the Bible says about our identity in Christ: "But as many as received Him, to them He gave the right to become children of God, even to those who believe in His name" (John 1:12). Who we are in Christ is extremely

1. Timothy Keller, as quoted by Joseph Sunde, "Timothy Keller on Work as Service vs. Idolatry," *Acton Institute Powerblog* (blog), December 12, 2012, http://blog.acton.org/archives/46741-timothy-keller-on-work-as-service-vs-idolatry.html.

important. This cannot be emphasized enough: our identity in Christ is crucial to our relationship with God and others. If we do not know who we are, we will always be striving for something we already have.

Our UPS driver has the right to my front door. However, he does not have the right to my bathroom, my kitchen, my living room, or my bedroom. But let's say my father comes to stay. He's going to sit on my couch, eat my food, use my bathroom, and sleep in my guest bedroom. My dad has rights because he's my dad. He's a family member.

We have rights as a child of God. God says we are part of his family. "Come in and make yourself comfortable. You are family."

Why does this matter when talking about conflict?

My family has conversations about our relationships that I'm not going to have with my UPS driver. My family is going to gather around the kitchen counter and talk about life. We can go into the presence of God the Father and talk about life because we're family. Our identity is in Christ—who we are, what we value, how we react to conflict. But when we're not part of that identity, or, like Pastor Jeremy, we forget to whom we belong, we are defenseless when conflict arises. We wallow in self-pity. We seek revenge. We seethe in anger. All of which gets in the way of being peacemakers.

The following are a number of identity statements found in the Bible. These verses will help you get your thinking correct. All of these statements are contingent on being a follower of Jesus. If you have not become a follower of Jesus, I encourage you to read them and reflect on what that relationship might offer you.

I am a friend of Jesus. "No longer do I call you slaves, for the slave does not know what his master is doing; but I have called you friends, for all things that I have heard from My Father I have made known to you" (John 15:15). Can you imagine? The Creator of the universe is your friend. You are God's friend. If you do not know Jesus, Jesus is also a friend of sinners. That amazes me as well. Jesus wants to be your friend even if you are still his enemy.

I am united with the Lord. "But the one who joins himself to the Lord is one spirit with Him" (1 Cor. 6:17). When disunity is spreading like gangrene in your life, be encouraged knowing that you are united with Jesus. This doesn't mean that Jesus necessarily supports your position in your conflict. But it does mean that you can unite with him. He is in you, and you can become one in spirit with him.

I am justified by faith. "Therefore, having been justified by faith, we have peace with God through our Lord Jesus Christ" (Rom. 5:1). I have come across many people who feel they are justified by perfect behavior. They will not say this, but their actions suggest as much. That's theologically wrong. You are justified by faith. The faith you have in the work Jesus did on the cross brings peace with God. Period.

What does it mean to be justified? You are declared righteous in the sight of God.

Believer, no matter what you have done or what you will do, you are justified because of—and only because of—Jesus Christ. Then some may ask, "Why repent?" We repent because we love God, not because we *want to be loved by God.* I love my wife; therefore, when I hurt her feelings, intentionally or accidentally, I ask her to forgive me. This is the same with God. We love him; therefore, we repent.

I am free from condemnation. "Therefore there is now no condemnation for those who are in Christ Jesus" (Rom. 8:1). Conflict doesn't condemn you. Tension doesn't send you to hell. Your relationship with God is condemnation-free because of Jesus Christ. When you are in a conflict with God or others, you may feel you stand condemned. You are not.

I want to warn you to distinguish between being convicted by the Holy Spirit and feeling condemned. Condemnation is a conviction of sin without hope; you feel no hope. Holy Spirit conviction is a conviction of sin with hope; you feel hope because it's really there. When we sin against God and others, the Holy Spirit is present, saying, "You did this wrong, but Jesus died for that. Repent."

I am sealed. "Now He who establishes us with you in Christ and anointed us is God, who also sealed us and gave us the Spirit in our hearts as a pledge" (2 Cor. 1:21–22). What is significant about being sealed? Think about sealing an envelope. You place your letter inside and seal the envelope. That letter is not going to get out on its own. The letter doesn't make the decision to leave the envelope. How much greater is God at sealing you with the Holy Spirit! You don't get unsealed by a little tension. You don't get unsealed because you have a fight with your spouse. You are sealed. You are anointed. You are established.

I have a secure love from God.

Who will separate us from the love of Christ? Will tribulation, or distress, or persecution, or famine, or nakedness, or peril, or sword? Just as it is written, "For your sake we are being put to death all day long; we were considered as sheep to be slaughtered." But in all these things we overwhelmingly conquer through Him who loved us. For I am convinced that neither death, nor life, nor angels, nor principalities, nor things present, nor things to come, nor powers, nor height, nor depth, nor any other created thing, will be able to separate us from the love of God, which is in Christ Jesus our Lord. (Rom. 8:35–39)

Conflict doesn't separate you from God's love. Tribulation doesn't separate you from God's love. God loves you no matter what your circumstances are. You are not just a conqueror; you are an overwhelming conqueror.

I am redeemed and forgiven. "In [Jesus] we have redemption, the forgiveness of sins" (Col. 1:14). In part 5, "Connect," we will go into more detail about forgiveness. Here I just want to mention that you have been bought. The price has been paid. You are not in a bartering system with God. Jesus redeemed you. He bought you. He paid the price. He paid it all with his life. He is your redemption.

I am complete. "In [Jesus] you have been made complete, and He is the head over all rule and authority" (Col. 2:10). When you are in a major battle, you may feel incomplete. When you argue with your spouse, you may feel incomplete. When you are disappointed with your friends, you may feel incomplete. Yet no matter the battle, argument, or disappointment, you are complete because of Jesus. The other person is complete because of Jesus.

There is something in us that continually says we are incomplete, there has got to be more. But the fact is that Jesus has made you complete. Self-righteousness does not make you complete. Jesus makes you complete. What would change if each morning you awoke and said, "I am complete"?

I am a member of Christ's body. "Now you are Christ's body, and individually members of it" (1 Cor. 12:27). You are Christ's body. This is a powerful statement. The context of this verse is spiritual gifts. The verse is talking about believers being part of the body of Christ. We often do not think about what happened in Christ's body.

Jesus Christ's body went to a cross. He was humiliated. He bled. He died. He was crucified.

Jesus Christ's body went to a grave. He was buried. His body lay in the grave for three days.

Jesus Christ's body resurrected. He came up out of the grave. He moved about on this earth.

Jesus Christ's body appeared. He appeared to many people as evidence of the resurrection.

Jesus Christ's body ascended. He ascended to the heavenly Father.

Here's the problem: many Christians want to be Christ's body without the cross. But that's impossible. You can't walk in the newness of life without experiencing the resurrection. You can't experience the resurrection without experiencing the crucifixion. You can't experience the crucifixion without experiencing the cross. That's why Jesus says in Matthew 16:24, "If anyone wishes to come after Me, he must deny himself, and take up his cross and follow Me." That's why Paul says in Romans 6:1–7:

> What shall we say then? Are we to continue in sin so that grace may increase? May it never be! How shall we who died to sin still live in it? Or do you not know that all of us who

have been baptized into Christ Jesus have been baptized into His death? Therefore we have been buried with Him through baptism into death, so that as Christ was raised from the dead through the glory of the Father, so we too might walk in newness of life. For if we have become united with Him in the likeness of His death, certainly we shall also be in the likeness of His resurrection, knowing this, that our old self was crucified with Him, in order that our body of sin might be done away with, so that we would no longer be slaves to sin; for he who has died is freed from sin.

This is critical to your identity. You are the body of Christ. You have spiritual gifts. You have been baptized into his death. You have been resurrected with him. You are freed from sin.

I am being finished. "For I am confident of this very thing, that He who began a good work in you will perfect it until the day of Christ Jesus" (Phil. 1:6). God has you in process. Do you allow yourself to be in process? In the middle of tension or conflict, do you demand perfection of yourself? Do you see improvement in how you handle conflict, or are you just trying to get even with the one you're in conflict with? God is faithful. He will finish you. Do not be discouraged. You are in good hands. He is making you more than you once were.

I am a citizen of heaven. "For our citizenship is in heaven, from which also we eagerly wait for a Savior, the Lord Jesus Christ" (Phil. 3:20). Your citizenship is in heaven. What does that mean? You are passing through this life. One day you will be in your home country, heaven. All the pains of being a foreigner will be gone. You will eventually arrive in the land of peace.

I am new. "Therefore if anyone is in Christ, he is a new creature; the old things passed away; behold, new things have come" (2 Cor. 5:17). What's defining you? Are you being defined by your past? Your heritage? Your ethnicity? Your employer? Your successes? Your failures? Many things may influence you, but God must *define* you. He says that you are new. He says that you are a new creature. He says that the old has passed away. That is why Paul says in Philippians 3:13–14, "Brethren, I do not regard myself as having laid hold of it yet; but one thing I do: forgetting what lies behind and reaching forward to what lies ahead, I press on toward the goal for the prize of the upward call of God in Christ Jesus."

Let go of the past. Choose not to remember it. Let God define your present. Let God define your identity. Press on to what God has called you to be.

I am God's workmanship. "For we are His workmanship, created in Christ Jesus for good works, which God prepared beforehand so that we would walk in them" (Eph. 2:10). God has prepared for you relationships in which you can reflect the gospel to others. He prepared these relationships before the foundations of the world. He desires that you walk in them. You were created in Christ Jesus. In a physical sense, your mom and dad conceived you; you were created in your mother's womb. In a spiritual sense, you were created in Jesus. Just as the womb is highly protective of a newly conceived baby, Jesus protects you and creates you for good works.

Our identity is in Christ. We're part of God's family, and he longs for us to embody his character. He is compassionate and gracious. He heals the brokenhearted. He will not despise a contrite heart. He is good. And he hears our prayers.

Who wouldn't want to follow a God like that? Who wouldn't want to incorporate the attributes of a God like that into their own life, particularly in times of conflict? And that, as we'll soon see, is our very calling as Christians: to be like him.

12

Living with an Eternal Perspective

Choose to view life through God's eyes. This will not be easy because it doesn't come naturally to us. We cannot do this on our own. We have to allow God to elevate our vantage point. Start by reading His Word, the Bible. . . . Pray and ask God to transform your thinking. Let Him do what you cannot. Ask Him to give you an eternal, divine perspective.

Charles Swindoll

How does understanding an eternal perspective during conflict bring about peace until reconciliation takes place? Doing so takes away the pressure of feeling that this is the only time and place that matter. Focusing on the eternal allows us to see God's safety net—eternity. Says 2 Corinthians 4:17–18, "For momentary, light affliction is producing for us an eternal weight of glory far beyond all comparison, while we look not at the things which are seen, but at the things which are not seen; for the things which are seen are temporal, but the things which are not seen are eternal."

Have you ever worked with someone who treated every decision in the workplace as a life-and-death matter? They probably did so because they'd made work, their career, and power their idols. They had a limited perspective about what really matters in life. But that's not the case with someone who also gives attention to family, friends, hobbies, or volunteer opportunities beyond the workplace. Christians, with the promise of eternal life, should have a broader perspective.

Remember how we talked about different people having different perspectives? Two people can look at the same facts but end up with different conclusions based on how each sees the world. We also talked about God's perspective in general. Now let's talk specifically about his eternal perspective.

Two primary ingredients make up an eternal perspective: First, where we fix our eyes. Second, what time frame we set our eyes on. We can reshape our stories by where we set our eyes; we can make tension positive or negative.

People ask how Tanya and I are able to care for our daughter, Isabella. First, we don't set our eyes on her disability. We set our eyes on the heavenly Father who entrusted a disabled daughter to us. Second, we don't fixate on the here and now. We will have more days with Isabella when she is whole and complete in heaven. We also imagine heaven being sweeter than earth, especially when we get to see our daughter dancing before the Lord.

Colossians 3:1–4 says, "Therefore if you have been raised up with Christ, keep seeking the things above, where Christ is, seated at the right hand of God. Set your mind on the things above, not on the things that are on earth. For you have died and your life is hidden with Christ in God. When Christ, who is our life, is revealed, then you also will be revealed with Him in glory."

Paul is telling us to seek the things above, to set our minds on them. How do we do that in the middle of relational tension? We will have more days whole and complete in heaven than we will have broken days here on earth. Does this mean we don't deal with the here and now? Of course not. But where we focus our minds is important. So many of us walk around with a fleeting perspective. We focus on the past. We focus on our failures. We focus on our limitations. Instead, we should lift up our eyes, look ahead, have an eternal perspective.

The choice is ours. In any given situation, we can look at the temporal or the eternal. In any given situation, we can look at passing pleasures or enduring ill-treatment. We always have a choice in our relationships. We always have a choice whether to take the easy path or the hard path. Consider Matthew 16:21–23: "From that time Jesus began to show His disciples that He must go to Jerusalem, and suffer many things from the elders and chief priests and scribes, and be killed, and be raised up on the third day. Peter took Him aside and began to rebuke Him, saying, 'God forbid it, Lord! This shall never happen to You.' But He turned and said to Peter, 'Get behind Me, Satan! You are a stumbling block to Me; for you are not setting your mind on God's interests, but man's.'"

Jesus had a view of ill-treatment and an eternal perspective. Peter had a view of passing pleasures and a temporal perspective.

Ephesians 4:17–24 says:

> So this I say, and affirm together with the Lord, that you walk no longer just as the Gentiles also walk, in the futility of their mind, being darkened in their understanding, excluded from the life of God because of the ignorance that is in them, because of the hardness of their heart; and they, having become callous, have given themselves over to sensuality for the practice of every kind of impurity with greediness. But you did not learn Christ in this way, if indeed you have heard Him and have been taught in Him, just as truth is in Jesus, that, in reference to your former manner of life, you lay aside the old self, which is being corrupted in accordance with the lusts of deceit, and that you be renewed in the spirit of your mind, and put on the new self, which in the likeness of God has been created in righteousness and holiness of the truth.

According to this passage, we think only of our own temporal interests instead of eternal interests when we do four things: embrace futile thinking, become darkened in our understanding, fill our minds with ignorance, and harden our hearts. Let's look at each one.

Futile thinking. Our minds are set on human interests when we embrace futile, fruitless, hopeless, and pointless thinking. Oftentimes during conflict, we think about pointless things. We begin to speculate and fill our hearts with hopelessness. This is a dangerous path for us to walk down.

The solution to futile thinking is to put on the new self, to proclaim the truths God has spoken about us. If you struggle with futile thinking, go back to the chapter on our identity in Christ (ch. 11) and look at the statements God makes about you. Keep in mind that the same statements apply to the person you are in conflict with.

Darkened understanding. Futile thinking leads to a darkened understanding. We speculate. We misinterpret our "goodness" and the thoughts of others. We block the truth of God's Word from our hearts.

The solution is the same as dealing with futile thinking. We must put on the new self. We must proclaim that the old man, the old woman has been put in the grave of the gospel. The newness of life runs through our veins.

Ignorant thinking. Maybe we aren't as deep into the Word as we need to be. Or maybe we understand the Word but have forgotten it, cast it aside, ignored it. Ignorant thinking is temporal thinking and will do nothing to solve whatever conflict we face.

Hardened hearts. Why is it that two people can sit in the same pew, week after week, hear the same message, and sing the same songs, and yet one goes out into the world with a heart for others and one goes out with a hardened heart? According to Ephesians, hardness comes from a mind focused on futility. Many Christians have lost the ability to show compassion to others. Why? They have lost an eternal perspective. They have looked at the futility of this world and thought, "This is it. What's the use? Why should I treat others with kindness?" They have forgotten that God is so much bigger than the here and now.

Again, we need to lay aside the old self and clothe ourselves with the new self. Romans 8:6–7 talks clearly about where we need to set our minds and the peace we can have. "For the mind set on the flesh is death, but the mind set on the Spirit is life and peace, because the mind set on the flesh is hostile toward God; for it does not subject itself to the law of God, for it is not even able to do so."

The mind set on the flesh—the old self—is death, hostile toward God. However, hope abounds. We must proclaim the Word of God in our minds, proclaim that we are children of God, proclaim that we are loved by God. What develops from this type of thinking? Life and peace. Life and peace are what every person is looking for in the world. How do we achieve it? We achieve life and peace by setting our minds on the Spirit. Look at what Jesus says: "But seek first His kingdom and His righteousness, and all these things will be added to you" (Matt. 6:33). If we seek first, or set our minds on, God's kingdom and God's righteousness, we will have everything we need. God doesn't limit this truth to our daily physical needs. It pours over into our relationship with God and our relationships with others. That's why we must be transformed by the renewing of our minds.

Romans 12:2 says, "And do not be conformed to this world, but be transformed by the renewing of your mind, so that you may prove what the will of God is, that which is good and acceptable and perfect." When our minds are transformed, we will prove the will of God. What is God's will? God's will is good. God's will is acceptable. God's will is perfect. If we hope to overcome conflict, we must realize we're doomed with our own inadequate tools. God's wisdom, love, and forgiveness must flow through us, and that can happen only when we look at any situation with an eternal, not a temporal, perspective.

13

Embracing Our Calling
to Be Peacemakers

*What you do in your house is worth as much as if you did
it in heaven for our Lord God.*

Martin Luther

When we take on the attributes of God—when God
lives in us through the Spirit, when the Spirit dwells
in us and produces God's characteristics—what do we become? Many things. But among them, peacemakers. We
become ambassadors with the mission of reconciling with
others because we've been reconciled to God.

Second Corinthians 5:17–21 says:

Therefore if anyone is in Christ, he is a new creature; the
old things passed away; behold, new things have come. Now
all these things are from God, who reconciled us to Himself
through Christ and gave us the ministry of reconciliation,

namely, that God was in Christ reconciling the world to Himself, not counting their trespasses against them, and He has committed to us the word of reconciliation.

Therefore, we are ambassadors for Christ, as though God were making an appeal through us; we beg you on behalf of Christ, be reconciled to God. He made Him who knew no sin to be sin on our behalf, so that we might become the righteousness of God in Him.

Paul starts out with the statement "If anyone is in Christ . . ." He starts out with a statement about who we are in Christ. He starts out with the substance of our faith, old to new. I love this about the Word of God. We are new. New things have come.

Then Paul moves into our responsibility. He says we have been given the ministry of reconciliation. Jesus talks about the same thing in the Sermon on the Mount. In fact, let's read the Beatitudes from the Sermon on the Mount to give context to what Jesus says in verse 9 specifically. Matthew 5:1–12 says:

When Jesus saw the crowds, He went up on the mountain; and after He sat down, His disciples came to Him. He opened His mouth and began to teach them, saying,
"Blessed are the poor in spirit, for theirs is the kingdom of heaven.
"Blessed are those who mourn, for they shall be comforted.
"Blessed are the gentle, for they shall inherit the earth.
"Blessed are those who hunger and thirst for righteousness, for they shall be satisfied.
"Blessed are the merciful, for they shall receive mercy.
"Blessed are the pure in heart, for they shall see God.
"Blessed are the peacemakers, for they shall be called sons of God.

"Blessed are those who have been persecuted for the sake of righteousness, for theirs is the kingdom of heaven.

"Blessed are you when people insult you and persecute you, and falsely say all kinds of evil against you because of Me. Rejoice and be glad, for your reward in heaven is great; for in the same way they persecuted the prophets who were before you."

Jesus places a high value on being poor in spirit, or humility. He says we are blessed when we mourn (over our sin). He identifies gentleness as a key characteristic for believers. He says we are to pursue righteousness, show mercy, have a pure heart. Then he says the line that we at Peacemaker Ministries love: "Blessed are the peacemakers."

Matthew 5:9 says, "Blessed are the peacemakers, for they shall be called sons of God." Jesus points out that peacemakers are part of the family of God. This statement means that all who are in the family of God and make peace in the name of Jesus are peacemakers.

What does God call peacemakers to do? Peacemakers are called to be humble, to mourn over their sins, to be gentle, to pursue righteousness, to give mercy, and to operate with pure motives. Most of all, peacemakers are to pursue peace.

God Calls Peacemakers to Be Pursuers

Romans 12:18 says, "If possible, so far as it depends on you, be at peace with all men."

God calls peacemakers to pursue peace with everyone. However, this verse is a great reminder that peace with everyone is not always an option. Let's break the verse down into three chunks.

"If Possible . . ."

Because we, as believers, are new creations in Christ, peace should always be possible. However, not everyone will be willing to reconcile or make peace. Sometimes making peace is not possible. Maybe the other person is unwilling or not ready. Still, we must be willing to pursue. I'm often asked, "Do I keep pursuing and pursuing?" How often you pursue or how long you pursue is dependent on what the Holy Spirit speaks to you. However, I believe you should always keep the door open to reconciliation. Let's say you make a request to reconcile a relationship and the other person turns you down. Don't turn bitter; instead, let them know you are always available.

"So Far as It Depends on You . . ."

We can make excuses why we don't pursue peace with someone else: "They'll never be willing to reconcile, so why bother? They're too stubborn. They're just *that* way." We aren't responsible for how people might react to our efforts at reconciliation. We *are* responsible for trying to reconcile.

"Be at Peace with All Men"

All of us can think of people with whom we have a broken relationship. These are the people we need to pursue. In the next chapter, we'll talk about some practical things to do prior to meeting with them. But let's face it, pursuing peace does not come naturally. Because of our sin nature, we seek revenge before we seek peace.

Overcome Evil with Good

Romans 12:19–21 says, "Never take your own revenge, be-loved, but leave room for the wrath of God, for it is written, 'Vengeance is Mine, I will repay,' says the Lord. 'But if your enemy is hungry, feed him, and if he is thirsty, give him a drink; for in so doing you will heap burning coals on his head.' Do not be overcome by evil, but overcome evil with good."

In other words, don't play God. He will take care of all injustices. This can be difficult for us to accept, but the reality is that God has his role and we have ours. We are not God. But that doesn't relieve us of responsibility. We have a com-mitment, and the passage tells us what it is: "If your enemy is hungry, feed him, and if he is thirsty, give him a drink."

If we've been wounded, getting revenge is often our first thought, and doing nothing is next in line. But going out of our way to help the one who has hurt us? Yes, we are to "overcome evil with good."

Spreading gossip is evil. For some reason, we think we need to share everything with everyone. Instead, we need to speak well of the person, bless the person who insults us. "But," you might say, "isn't that like telling a lie?" Let me share what Jesus and Peter have to say about the matter. In Matthew 5:10–12, Jesus says, "Blessed are those who have been persecuted for the sake of righteousness, for theirs is the kingdom of heaven. Blessed are you when people insult you and persecute you, and falsely say all kinds of evil against you because of Me. Rejoice and be glad, for your reward in heaven is great; for in the same way they persecuted the prophets who were before you." And Peter says in 1 Peter 3:8–9, "To sum up, all of you be harmonious, sympathetic, brotherly, kindhearted, and humble in spirit; not returning evil for evil or insult for insult, but giving a blessing instead; for you were called for the very purpose that you might inherit a blessing."

When people don't want to reconcile, we need to give them a blessing instead. We are blessed when we are willing to reconcile and they are not willing. So instead of cursing them to our spouse or friend, we need to give a blessing, not write them off, and always be looking for opportunities to try to make a reconnection.

Reconciliation Comes First

"If they have a problem with me, then they need to come and talk to me," people often say. Such a statement is often grounded in pride and not consistent with what Scripture teaches in Matthew 5:23–24: "Therefore if you are presenting your offering at the altar, and there remember that your brother has something against you, leave your offering there before the altar and go; first be reconciled to your brother, and then come and present your offering."

During the greeting time at church, I was shaking a man's hand when I discerned something was not right between the two of us. Sure enough, as soon as I let go of his hand, he stormed out of the service. I was not preaching that day, so I went looking for him in the building. I found him sitting in our café.

"Do we need to talk?" I asked.

"Sure."

We went to my office, where he unloaded a story about how we had not been there to help him in a time of need.

"We were being evicted, and you and the church didn't care," he said.

I listened. "I'm sorry," I said. "I truly am. Do you mind if I share a different perspective?"

"Sure," he said. "Share it with me."

I told him the church *did* know of his need and wanted to help, but we needed a definitive dollar amount of his need. "We couldn't just give cash," I said.

At that, he shifted the focus of his hurt a bit. "Well, no one helped my family move. I put it on a prayer request card, and no one followed up."

"Again, I'm sorry," I said. "I was unaware of this."

He got mad and stormed out.

The incident highlights two biblical principles. First, Matthew 5:23–24 says that even "at the altar" we are to go and seek reconciliation if we sense a rift between us and someone else. I did so. Second, Romans 12:18 says that we are to live at peace with others "so far as it depends on you." In other words, we need to do all we can to bring about peace, but we must understand that it's a two-way street. I thought that by talking with the man we could heal the rift. But in the end, his anger got the best of him. Even then, I continued to seek peace. I went to his wife and explained the situation. She understood.

"I would be happy to sit down with both of you and work this out," I said.

"I'm not offended," she said. "I'll see what my husband wants to do."

Months later, this man and I were able to sit down. I was able to apologize for not serving him well as his pastor, and he was able to apologize for blowing up. We both forgave each other, and God got the glory.

The fact that God would have us interrupt a worship service to be reconciled with someone underscores how important he believes being at peace with others is. If we are worshiping and remember our spouse is mad at us, we need to stop worshiping and go be reconciled to him or her. When we do so, we glorify God.

Looking Out for the Interests of Others

And what if we believe someone has sinned against us? Matthew 18:15 says, "If your brother sins, go and show him his fault in private; if he listens to you, you have won your brother."

Many of us fail to keep others' offenses private. We tend to tell everyone but the person with whom we're having the problem. Here's the litmus test as to whether our pride is getting the best of us: when we are willing to be harshly critical of someone who's not physically present, pride is rearing its ugly head. We have a problem.

A friend's church had a terrible split. He wrote a passionate letter to the elder board in which he pointed out the faults of a particular pastor. Later, he was at a mall when he thought, "I hope I don't run into that pastor's wife." While contemplating why that should bother him, he realized his letter had been fueled by pride and intended to heap scorn on the pastor. Instead of being a means to bring about peace, the letter was a means of bringing about punishment. His conscience bothered him for good reason. Regardless of the pastor's role in the church split, my friend had to deal with his own sin. My friend wasn't trying to initiate reconciliation; he was out for revenge. He wasn't looking out for the interests of others; he was seeking satisfaction for himself.

Peacemakers are called to look out for the interests of others. Philippians 2:1–11 says:

> Therefore if there is any encouragement in Christ, if there is any consolation of love, if there is any fellowship of the Spirit, if any affection and compassion, make my joy complete by being of the same mind, maintaining the same love, united in spirit, intent on one purpose. Do nothing from selfishness or empty conceit, but with humility of mind regard one another as more important than yourselves; do not merely look out for your own personal interests, but also for the interests of others. Have this attitude in yourselves which was also in Christ Jesus, who, although He existed in the form of God, did not regard equality with God a thing to be grasped, but emptied Himself, taking the form of a bond-servant, and being made in the likeness of men. Being found in appearance as a man, He humbled Himself by becoming obedient to the point of death, even death on a cross. For this reason also, God highly exalted Him, and bestowed on Him the name which is above every name, so that at the name of Jesus EVERY KNEE WILL BOW, of those who are in heaven and on earth and under the earth, and that every tongue will confess that Jesus Christ is Lord, to the glory of God the Father.

Look at this list from Paul, who challenges us to something that's far beyond our natural ability:

- Be of the same mind.
- Maintain the same love.
- Be united in spirit.
- Be intent on one purpose.

- Don't be selfish.
- Regard others as more important than yourself.

Think of someone with whom you've had a falling out. If you emptied yourself and served the other person's interests, what would change in your relationship? What if you humbled yourself and let God exalt you? Something amazing would come out of your life. But something amazing happens only when we humble ourselves before God and others, when we act with godly motives, when we dare to look deeply into the mirror. Proverbs 16:2 says, "All the ways of a man are clean in his own sight, but the Lord weighs the motives."

Therein is the key to every contentious relationship in which we find ourselves: we all have blind spots. A blind spot is something we can't see on our own. There are only three ways to figure out our blind spots:

- God will reveal them to us through his Word and through the Holy Spirit.
- God will reveal them to us through life circumstances.
- God will reveal them to us through someone else.

But all these revelations depend on our willingness to reflect. That's the next step in the process of reconciliation and part 4 of this book. Knowing there's tension in the world, knowing our stories, knowing others' stories, and knowing who God is and who we are in him are integral to the process. However, such steps are meaningless if we can't reflect on where we are spiritually and where we need to be.

PART 4
REFLECT

14

Search Me, O Lord

A prayer God will always answer is "Search me."

Pastor Tim Yetter

A friend of mine, one of those children of the sixties, was telling me about the biggest mistake he'd made in starting a garage band back in the day and how his own son had repeated a similar mistake a generation later. "With my own band, we spent all day arguing about what our name was going to be," he said. "That was our priority—the name. With my son's band, in the 1990s, they came up with a name in a hurry but spent all day creating a website to extol the virtues of the band. That was their priority—promoting themselves as amazing musicians. We both overlooked something fairly important in the process."

"What was that?" I asked.

"We didn't ask a hard question of ourselves: Are any of us the least bit qualified to play music? The answer at our first—and only—practice was no. Not by a long shot."

When the challenge is bringing peace to stressful situations, people tend to gravitate toward one of two poles. Lacking courage, they run from trying to interact with another person or group. In other words, they're afraid to even start the band. They are afraid to learn or practice the music together. Or lacking self-reflection, they attack and never allow any significant self-examination to see if they are ready to reconcile. As would-be peacemakers, they begin interacting with a person or group they've had a falling-out with long before they're ready. In other words, they're so anxious to start the process that they forget the real priority: the music, the heart of the matter.

Music is reflective. So, too, is peacemaking—or, at least, it should be. We have looked at our relationship with God. We have ascended. We have established who we are in Christ. We have established the character and presence of God. We have looked at an eternal perspective. We have evaluated our calling. In other words, we've done much to spiritually prepare ourselves to be peacemakers. But before we begin the hard work of reconciliation, we need to do the hard work of reflection.

Thus far we've been talking about being, and now we're talking about doing. But returning to our music metaphor, this action step isn't about stepping up on stage and wailing on the guitar or the drums. Quite the opposite. It's about stepping back to a place where there is no audience but a more experienced musician and mustering the courage to ask, "Could I be playing some dissonant notes that are

leading to disunity in the band's music? Could I have some
blind spots?"

Nobody likes to subject themselves to revelations that
can make them uncomfortable; they're hard on the ego. No
musician likes to have a bandmate or mentor stop midnote
and say, "No, no, no. More like *this*." But that's what makes
a musician better. And that's what will make our quest to
find peace with others better.

Search Me

Our first request of God in self-reflection is to search us.
This is like playing in front of a musician who knows far
more about our instrument than we could ever hope to and
saying, "Tell me what I can improve." We know the process
will be painful. But we know it will help our music be far
better than it otherwise would have been.

Think about people you know who are somehow stuck
in life. Often what holds them up is their unwillingness to
search their hearts—and let God search their hearts—to see
what blind spots they might be experiencing. They blame
others. They blame God. And in so doing, they put off the
difficult but fruitful task of better understanding themselves.
Which keeps them from being peacemakers.

Going back to the prodigal son and the older brother, the
prodigal, though rebellious and stubborn early on, came to
his senses and ultimately welcomed God to search him and
guide him. Doing so changed his life. The older brother,
meanwhile, did not and embraced a life of bitterness.

Psalm 139 is a powerful chapter that expresses God's knowl-
edge of each of us and the psalmist giving God permission to

search him. The psalm is broken into two parts: search me, then teach me. The first four verses read, "O Lord, You have searched me and known me. You know when I sit down and when I rise up; You understand my thought from afar. You scrutinize my path and my lying down, and are intimately acquainted with all my ways. Even before there is a word on my tongue, behold, O Lord, You know it all." Later, in verses 23–24, the psalmist writes, "Search me, O God, and know my heart; try me and know my anxious thoughts; and see if there be any hurtful way in me, and lead me in the everlasting way."

Teach Me

Most of Psalm 139 is an affirmation that God knows us far better than we know ourselves and far better than anyone else knows us. But at the end of it, the author shifts from "Examine my ways" to "Teach me your ways." The Message says it like this: "Investigate my life, O God, find out everything about me; cross-examine and test me, get a clear picture of what I'm about; see for yourself whether I've done anything wrong—then guide me on the road to eternal life" (vv. 23–24).

What's most important in this process of reflection is to remember God's purpose. It isn't to beat us up. It isn't to shame us. It isn't to make us feel like a worthless sack of flesh and bones. Instead, God desires to help us become more than we were in our bitterness. He wants to help us play a part in his drama of bringing reconciliation to a world that doesn't want reconciliation. He wants to help us refrain from what our natural instinct might be in these situations: pointing a finger at the other person and demanding that they think, react, and change. News flash: we can't control the other person. We can only control our own actions, and even then, we can only control our own actions with limited success, given our sin nature.

God is saying, OK, *in your journey, you've done well here and here and here . . . but do you see how you took a wrong turn here? That may well have skewed your perspective regarding your relationship with so-and-so. Once you understand that, you'll be better equipped when you go to that person to try to mend the rift you have made.*

A sixtyish woman I'll call Linda walked up to me in the church foyer. Six months earlier, her grown daughter had told her that she could not see her grandchildren again. Linda was in turmoil. Her daughter wouldn't return her calls. Linda would text—no answer. She would swing by her daughter's house, and even though their cars were there, her daughter wouldn't answer the door. The harder Linda pushed, the further away her daughter retreated. Linda looked me in the eye with tears running down her cheeks.

"What should I do?" she asked.

I knew the drill, both in my own life and in the lives of those I had counseled.

"Linda, I would like you to read Psalm 139:23–24," I said, "then come back next week and tell me what it says."

The next week she returned, having read the psalm.

"And what does it say?" I asked.

"That I should ask God to search me."

"Good. This week read that psalm every day, asking God to search you."

She agreed to do it and returned the next week.

"OK, I did it. I read it every day."

"And what did God speak to your heart either through Scripture or through the Holy Spirit?"

"God led me to Psalm 27:14, which says, 'Wait for the LORD.' But what do you think I should do?"

"Linda, if God told you to wait for him, who am I to tell you differently? If I were you, I would wait on the Lord."

Every week for about a month she came back, and every week I asked her what Scripture or the Holy Spirit had led her to do. Every week she said the same thing: "God has told me to wait." And every week I responded, "Then you should wait."

At the end of a month, the daughter called Linda and said she wanted to get together. She wanted to share the grandkids with Linda. Linda was ecstatic. Her waiting on God had taken the pressure off her daughter, and that had led to some self-examination on the young woman's part. God had been working on her daughter, and mother and daughter were finally reunited.

Some people might think waiting is a cop-out, an avoidance of the problem at hand, a fleeing from the real issue. But do you see what happened here? Linda's waiting allowed some reflection to occur in her daughter and in herself. Sometimes we are the ones who need to correct our ways, and sometimes another person or group needs to correct their ways. But none of that can happen if we rush to judgment. None of that can happen if we don't allow God time to look inside us and become part of the solution.

Do you see what didn't happen here? Linda didn't attack her daughter, didn't accuse her, didn't put the pressure on her to make things right, didn't try to control her. And, like the prodigal son, her daughter ultimately came to her senses. But that can take time.

Remember the psalmist's plea: "God, search me. God, reveal to me. God, lead me." At the first sign of a falling-out with someone, what an amazing difference turning to this verse would make—and then acting on it, even if it meant waiting.

15

The Power of Overlooking

Be hard on yourself and easy on others. Carry your own cross but never lay one on the back of another.

A. W. Tozer

William and Steve's friendship had spanned nearly three decades. Now, as Steve prepared for his daughter's late-December wedding, he asked William if he could borrow his friend's van to haul some decorative items to the church for the wedding. William didn't have to think twice. They were brothers in Christ. They routinely helped each other out. They could bare their souls to each other. "All yours," said William. But what seemed like a no-brainer response— take my van, please—became the catalyst for something that could have strained, even ended, their friendship.

While driving the van, Steve was attempting to cross a busy, four-lane highway when another car collided with the van. Steve wasn't hurt, nor was the driver of the other car, but both vehicles were totaled. Though Steve believed the person driving the other car was exceeding the speed limit, the police determined that he was at fault; the other driver had the right-of-way. What's more, William's insurance company informed him that, in their eyes, who was driving the van was irrelevant. "The insurance," the agent said, "follows the owner of the vehicle, not the driver. Sorry, William, but you're liable."

Before I share how the story ended, I'd like to share how it could have ended. Despite the insurance company's determination that William was responsible for the financial repercussions from the accident, he could have said, "How fair is that? I wasn't driving. How could I be responsible? In fact, it was only through my generosity that Steve was driving in the first place. And now look, I'm the one who's going to have to waste valuable time finding another vehicle and paying for his mistake. He's my friend, sure, but friendship isn't going to pay my bills. The wreck was his fault; the officer even said so. Steve is responsible for any financial liability, period."

And Steve, if he were the blame-others type, could have said, "Hey, it wasn't my fault that the woman who hit me was speeding. I've crossed that highway dozens of times in the same scenario and never been hit. If William's twenty-year-old van had a little more power, that never would have happened. I would've gotten out of the way. The insurance company has already ruled that I'm not responsible. William is."

That's not, in fact, how the story played out. Steve's initial thoughts were of two people: his daughter and William. Before the wreckers had even towed the vehicles away and while still in semishock, he reminded himself that his daughter was the priority. The wedding was only two days away, and he didn't want the accident to steal her joy in any manner. And in a phone call from the accident scene, Steve apologized profusely to William for what had happened. "I'm so sorry. I'll pay for any deductible your insurance won't cover."

When Steve made that call, William's first question was, "Are you OK?" He was relieved to find that Steve hadn't been hurt. But that's just the first half of the story. As William made his way to the accident scene, his good-naturedness began deteriorating. He was out both money and time, of which he had little. He was juggling not two but three jobs. He hadn't even owned the van for a year; it had replaced another one that had broken down before Christmas the previous year. He was a busy man with a limited budget. It had taken him nearly a month to find the now-banged-up van, and he was going to have to go through the same hardship again. *How hard is it to cross a highway in a perfectly good vehicle? I don't need this, God. Why now? Why me?*

Then as the prodigal son did, he came to his senses. *Hold on, pal. Put yourself in Steve's shoes. A bad thing happened to a great guy, a great guy whose daughter is getting married in two days. She needs to be the priority. Your friendship with Steve needs to be the priority. That van is just a hunk of metal on four rubber tires. More important things are at play. God, help Steve and his family overcome this. Thank you nobody was hurt. And please help his daughter to have a great wedding on Saturday.*

William arrived at the scene and tried to comfort an obviously distraught Steve. William tried to put Steve at ease even as Steve kept apologizing and assuring William that he'd cover any financial liability. "Hey, don't worry about it," said

William. "Let's focus on Saturday. Let's not let this get in the way of your daughter having a great wedding, my friend."

Words are one thing; money is another. A week later, the insurance company called with good news. The liability portion of William's insurance would pay fully to compensate the other driver, compensate him fair-market value for his van, and require only a $500 deductible.

"I'll pay for that," Steve insisted. "I was driving."

"No, you won't," William said. "It's my responsibility."

Steve didn't have to offer to pay the $500; after all, the letter of the law—at least the insurance company's law—had determined that William was responsible. William, meanwhile, didn't have to forgive the $500; after all, the spirit of the law—not to mention the police—suggested Steve was at fault. What's more, $500 wasn't all that much for Steve to pay, and he'd offered to do so. William could have simply accepted the money, but instead he stood firm. He refused Steve's offer to pay. Meanwhile, the wedding wasn't the least bit spoiled by the accident. In essence, this was one of those happily ever after stories.

Why did the story have a happy ending? Because both men exemplified a biblical principle about overlooking an offense to prioritize something they saw as more important than money, justice, or revenge: their friendship. Says Proverbs 19:11, "Good sense makes one slow to anger, and it is his glory to overlook an offense" (ESV).

Overlooking Offenses

An offense can be many things, from a simple comment to a physical assault. By definition, overlooking an offense is intentionally choosing not to hold on to hurt or to judge a person who has hurt us or someone else. It's a tool, a way to keep a situation from getting worse, a way not to let bitterness eat away at us when we are offended. But please don't confuse overlooking with denial. Overlooking is choosing not to pursue judgment against another person or to hold on to an injustice. Denial, on the other hand, is pretending an offense didn't take place when it did or pretending an offense didn't hurt when it did.

Overlooking offenses is appropriate in the following situations:

- The offense did not create a wall between us and the other person or cause us to feel differently toward them for more than a short period of time.
- The offense did not cause serious harm (to us, to the offender, to others, or to God's reputation).
- The offense was isolated and not part of a destructive pattern of behavior.

If your spouse is cheating on you, their decision to do so has created a wall between you that overlooking is not going to solve. In such a case, don't overlook the offense. On the other hand, if a friend has a habit of butting in on conversations you're having with others but your friendship with this person is otherwise strong, their actions should not destroy your relationship. Unless this is a continual habit that seriously threatens your friendship, in most cases, you can overlook it.

Whether or not a hurt can be overlooked often depends on the truths about the situation, how much hurt we're carrying, and how much baggage we have. Let's look at three examples.

Example 1. A wife and husband get into a heated discussion about politics, and she is hurt. After reflecting, she determines four things: *(1) we typically don't fight about politics; (2) we both had long days; (3) I don't think it will happen again; and (4) I forgive because God forgives me.* Response: overlook. Move on.

Example 2. A wife and husband get into a heated discussion about politics, and he calls her an idiot. What are the truths she knows about the situation? The four mentioned above plus one more: *I need to let him know calling me a name hurt.* Why? Because among the truths she's carrying is this: *Every morning I think about him calling me a name, and it hurts.* Response: don't overlook. She needs to be honest with her husband so that he understands how such comments add up and make her feel inadequate, insignificant, and hurt.

Example 3. A wife and husband get into a heated discussion about politics, and he calls her an idiot. In response, she storms out of the house and is gone for three days. Her truth: *Every morning I think about him calling me a name, and it hurts.* His truth: *She's been gone for three days, and I'm worried.* Her response: *I need to let him know calling me a name hurt. But before I do that, I need to take responsibility for leaving the house and worrying him for three days.* His response: *I need to apologize for calling her an idiot and pledge not to let that happen again.*

An Additional Tool to Overlooking

Beyond overlooking, another tool we can use to help resolve conflict is perspective. This goes back to what we talked about in part 2 about understanding our stories and the story of the other person. Perspective helps us see a conflict more clearly. Perspective helps us see the bigger picture and adds potential for bringing about peace.

Remember the discussion of 1 Samuel 16:7 regarding how the Lord looked at leadership qualities in a different way than how we might? "But the LORD said to Samuel, 'Do not look at his appearance or at the height of his stature, because I have rejected him; for God sees not as man sees, for man looks at the outward appearance, but the LORD looks at the heart.'"

If we look at a conflict from only our own, selfish perspective, the potential for ruining the relationship is great. We need to look instead at other perspectives in addition to our own. We must also look at the facts of the conflict. If how we react in a situation is influenced by the ten factors discussed earlier (view of God, childhood, church experience, etc.), we should filter our reaction and the other person's reaction through those factors. Hopefully, we will reach a new perspective that will give us peace in the relationship.

Let's again define all the perspectives that may come into play in a conflict:

- your perspective: your story plus your interpretation of your story plus your healthy or unhealthy response to the tension you are experiencing
- the other person's perspective: their story plus their interpretation of their story plus their healthy or unhealthy response to the tension they are experiencing
- your shared perspective: the common ground you have with the other person

151

- God's perspective: how your heavenly Father sees the situation; God's perspective is viewed through his Son Jesus Christ
- an eternal perspective: how you see the situation through the lens of eternity
- your new perspective: the result of you objectively considering all perspectives and beginning to understand the other person's interpretation of events (i.e., putting yourself in the other person's shoes)

Let's say there's tension in your household about money. Your perspective: money is tight. God's perspective: I own everything. Your new perspective: God is our Provider; we'll be fine. Relax.

Let's say a friend sinned against you. Your friend has asked for forgiveness, but you are still angry and hurt. Your perspective: my friend intentionally sinned against me, and I don't want to forgive them. God's perspective: Jesus died for that friend; Jesus forgives that friend. Your new perspective: I should forgive my friend because God has forgiven both me and my friend.

Let's say John has lost hope for his marriage. He wants to give up. He doesn't believe his wife will ever change and blames her for their problems. His perspective: I've lost hope for my marriage. Eternal perspective: every relationship is made whole in heaven. John's new perspective: I'll wait to see what God is going to do between now and eternity to show the gospel to me and my spouse.

It's important to contrast your perspective with God's perspective. It's also important to contrast your perspective with that of the other person. By doing so, you'd be surprised by how much you have in common; that is what is called "shared perspective." Getting from conflict to peace takes a fair amount of vulnerability on both people's part. I've been there. Now remember that overlooking an incident is not pretending it didn't happen. It's not denial. Instead, it's acknowledging something happened but instead of interacting with the person in an attempt to find peace with them, we keep the offense just between us and God and move on. We don't let it define the relationship.

The following story is one I never shared with the other person; I chose, instead, to overlook the offense. I chose to lay my hurt before the cross and move forward. It's about my daughter, Isabella, and her disability. I have a close friend I'll call Carl. He walked with me through discovering Isabella's disability. At that time, I was hurting deeply about Isabella's disability. I was frustrated by the path that was unfolding before me. And thus I was hypersensitive to anything regarding the health of my children.

Carl's wife was pregnant with their first child. "I'm excited that my wife is pregnant," Carl told me one day. "As long as the baby is happy, healthy, and whole, we will be good."

His words slammed me like a tsunami. By his logic, if he and his wife would be "good" only if their baby was born happy, healthy, and whole, then my wife and I must be "bad" because our baby wasn't born healthy. And because our daughter has an incurable disease, I guess my wife and I are destined to have bad lives.

I know Carl didn't intentionally try to hurt me; he made the statement in the context of his own situation, not mine. But it still wounded me. For days, the comment replayed in my mind. And for days, I felt resentment toward Carl. I debated whether to go to him. The answer seemed to be to stop, pray, and overlook the offense. "Lord," I prayed, "my friend said something that I'm particularly sensitive to right now. I know Carl didn't mean it the way I took it, but I was offended. So I lay it down at the cross, and I will let you heal the hurt I am feeling. Lord, thank you for healing me."

And he did. In God's eternal perspective, this was not a fall-on-your-sword offense. My friendship with Carl remains strong to this day, in part, I believe, because God gave me the power to overlook the offense. It's a power we all need to develop unless we want to live lives dogged by bitterness.

16

Of Logs and Specks

We should be rigorous in judging ourselves and gracious in judging others.

John Wesley

When Edward first smelled what seemed like someone's sweaty workout clothes and shoes left in a company locker room, he glanced at the sign on the wall—"No workout attire left overnight in lockers"—and shook his head. He looked at the locker next to his. *What's wrong with people?*

The second time, with the smell even more pungent, he mentally confronted the mystery culprit with an imaginary tongue-lashing on basic workplace etiquette: *Look, pal, whoever you are, it's pretty simple. Bring your clothes in the morning. Work out. Take them home at night. Wash. Repeat. It's not rocket science. Instead, you've obviously locked your clothes in a locker next to mine, use them day after day, and never wash them. Works for you, not for me.*

The third time, with the smell having ripened into a stench that Edward could hardly stand, he decided to report the violator to human resources. This guy was going to pay. Edward went to stuff his workout bag in what he thought was an empty locker before heading upstairs to HR but realized it had clothes in it. Some really smelly clothes. Some really smelly clothes that—wait a second, how could this be?—looked a lot like they belonged to, uh, him.

Oh my. It all came back to him. A few weeks before, he'd forgotten to take his workout clothes and shoes home one day, so he had brought fresh ones the next day. Then he'd forgotten all about the first batch. And all this time he was ready to have the culprit prosecuted to the full extent of the company law. Now he had to face the reality that he was the guilty party.

Laugh about the incident if you will, but isn't this how many conflicts play out? We're so busy being steamed about the perceived wrongdoings of someone else that we never stop to consider that the wrongdoer might be us. Matthew 7:4–5 nails this idea on the head: "How can you say to your brother, 'Let me take the speck out of your eye,' and behold, the log is in your own eye? You hypocrite, first take the log out of your own eye, and then you will see clearly to take the speck out of your brother's eye."

Our sin nature guarantees that we don't see ourselves objectively. We see ourselves through self-colored glasses. And too often we see others with judgmental eyes. "The average Christian is the most piercingly critical individual known," wrote Oswald Chambers nearly a century ago.[1] Not much

1. Oswald Chambers, "Beware of Criticizing Others," *My Utmost for His Highest*, June 17, https://utmost.org/beware-of-criticizing-others/.

has changed. Seeing the faults of others is easy. Seeing our own faults is sometimes all but impossible.

The Log-and-Speck Tool

This tendency is all the more reason why we need to pay close attention to the next tool in our toolbox for dealing with conflict: the log-and-speck tool. First, some terminology. A log is sinful behavior, intentional or unintentional, that we see in ourselves—behavior we need to repent of. A speck is the sinful behavior, intentional or unintentional, that we see in others.

We can deal with logs and specks in two ways: proactively identify the logs in our lives over which we have a tendency to stumble or reactively respond to tension we may have already created by concentrating on the specks we see in others' lives instead of the log in our own eyes. In either case, self-reflection is necessary. In fact, I recommend four steps of self-reflection:

Step 1: Pray and ask the Holy Spirit to reveal to you your logs and your contribution to the tension you have experienced—an extension of "Search me, O Lord."

Step 2: Make a list of all the things the Holy Spirit reveals to you.

Step 3: Make a list of all the ways the other person has sinned against you.

Step 4: Review the lists. If you're spiritually grounded, if you're living with an eternal perspective, if you're allowing the Holy Spirit to knead into your life the same kind of humility that allowed the prodigal son to run to his father, then your list of logs should be way longer than the list of specks of the other person.

Does this mean they're better than you, that you're inferior? Not at all. It means you have a God's-eye perspective on your life—and that's healthy. It means you have the potential to become more Christlike. It means you are maturing in your walk with Christ. Do not dwell on better or worse comparisons; that's a no-win proposition.

Hypothetically, let's say a father ponders his shortcomings in regard to his children. As he starts his assessment, the only thing that comes to mind is the way he's sinned against them. Is he done with the process? Hardly. Now it's time to allow the Holy Spirit to dig deeper, to shine the light of perspective on places his pride hasn't allowed light to reach. So he prays, and this is what's revealed to him regarding logs and specks:

Kids' Speck List
Did not listen.
Disrespectful.

His Log List
Yelled.
Was impatient.
Tried to gain respect through disrespectful means.
Did not take into account that what they were doing in their eyes didn't warrant a serious scolding.
Left the room angry.
Let the sun go down on his anger.

Did not correct with gentleness. (God's Word says in Romans 2:4 that God's kindness leads us to repentance; the father's behavior suggested that he thought loudness would do so for his kids.)

Did not model the heavenly Father well.

Became impatient with his wife as a result of his anger.

In the end, he wasn't angry with his kids or his wife, but he took it out on them. He was actually angry at himself for responding to his children so poorly. That's a US National Forest worth of logs. But we don't see the forest for the trees unless we welcome in the Holy Spirit and are genuinely open to seeing our sin. Of course, it's not our nature to do so. Nor is it our culture's nature. "Never let 'em see you sweat," says the TV advertisement. "Don't blame us," says one political party. "Blame the other party" (while, of course, the other party is saying the same thing). "I didn't touch the guy!" yells the football defensive back who was just flagged for pass interference—as the video replay shows he not only touched the guy but also grabbed his jersey and shoved him out of bounds to prevent him from catching the pass.

Assume You Could Be Part of the Problem

In terms of solving conflicts with others, we won't get anywhere if we don't, at first, assume that we could be part of the problem, maybe a big part. We can't be like the person who is anxious to get counseling so that the counselor can exonerate them and blame everything on their spouse. Our default instead needs to be, "I'm responsible for me, and I will undoubtedly have some issues to work on."

A youth basketball coach became increasingly frustrated by the actions of the coach of a Christian school that was beating his team by forty points. Even though his team was ahead, the coach of the Christian team would argue calls. "My guy was fouled in the act of shooting!" he'd yell at the referee. "He should get two shots, not a one-and-one!" Although his team was playing splendidly, he would berate his players as if a forty-point lead was insufficient, kick the bench, and stomp around. In short, he was anything but a good role model of a Christian school or of Christ himself. And the assistant coach was acting nearly as badly as the head coach.

As the last seconds ticked off the clock, the coach of the losing team felt the anger welling up inside him. He was trying to be a salt-and-light example to the unbelieving parents of his own team's players while the coach of the Christian team behaved so poorly. Why would any of his kids' parents want anything to do with Christianity after watching this supposed representative of Christ?

When the buzzer sounded to end the game, he raced to midcourt, and instead of shaking the winning coach's hand, he said to him, "How can you even sleep at night, acting like that?"

"What are you talking about?"

"Yelling, screaming, kicking the bench—what kind of testimony is that?"

"Hey, pal," said the winning coach, whose assistant stood by with the same kind of defiance, "take the log out of your eye first—look at how wigged out you are yourself—and then come see me."

The moment was not Christianity at its best. Both men had failed. Both had logs in their eyes. The coach of the winning team had lost perspective of what's most important; he valued winning and power and pride over others—fans, referees, opposing players, the opposing coach, even his own team. Like the prodigal son, he'd lost his way.

The coach of the losing team, however, wasn't blameless. Though he had every reason to be frustrated with the actions of the other coach, he had lost perspective on how to best handle conflict. In his self-righteousness, trying to be salt and light for the unbelieving parents, he had allowed his anger to get the best of him at game's end and had immediately antagonized the winning coach. Like the older brother, he'd also lost his way.

Speaking of the prodigal son and the older brother, let's look back at the two men from Luke who have already made some guest appearances in these pages. Each had a log in his eye. Only one, however, had the courage to realize it.

When the prodigal son took his father's inheritance and squandered it on sinful living, he exhibited what we might call self-centered actions. Self-centered actions are heart attitudes, words, or behaviors that lead us down an immoral path to gratify our sinful cravings.

On the other hand, the older brother exhibited what we might call self-righteous actions. Self-righteous actions are heart attitudes, words, or behaviors that lead us down a self-righteous path *not* to gratify sinful cravings. Neither is where we want to be. Both are about self, not about God and others.

But here's the good news that, by now, I hope you're picking up on: we don't have to remain chained to our sin. Jesus died on the cross for our sin, not so we can live stagnant lives, quietly gloating that we're saved while living totally for self (see the prodigal son before his change and the older brother throughout the story), but so we can know the Holy Spirit's power and change (see the prodigal son after he came to his senses). God is less concerned about who we've been than about who we might be. But reaching the potential of the latter necessitates looking at ourselves in the mirror and being willing to see weaknesses that we can overcome. The prodigal son examined himself, and doing so changed his life. The older brother did not, and the last we see of him, he was living a life of bitterness.

Self-Centered and Self-Righteous Living

Think about the prodigal son's self-centered living. What would go on his log list? Now think about the older brother's self-righteous living. What would go on his log list? Of course, listing the weaknesses of others is always more fun, but that's part of the problem here, right? We're quick to see the faults in others and slow to see the faults in ourselves. This has probably created some tension in our lives, but it is tension we want to use to help us become more Christ-centered and equipped for conflict.

How can you turn that negative tension into positive tension, from a disadvantage into an advantage? There are two steps:

Step 1: Ask the Holy Spirit to convict you of all self-centered actions and self-righteous actions. Ask God to help you come to your senses.

Step 2: Write down the ways you have walked in self-centered or self-righteous ways.

Let's say Bob gives false flattery to his boss in order to get a raise. Bob continually takes ten to twenty extra minutes on his breaks, but when confronted about it, he lies to his boss, claiming he was working. His self-centered action was taking extra-long breaks. His self-righteous actions were pretending to be an awesome employee by gushing about his boss and lying about working when he wasn't.

Sue doesn't study for her college finals. She then tells her parents she was sick and that's why she failed a class. Her self-centered actions were not studying and lying to her parents about being sick.

Frank is always twenty minutes early to work. At home, he continually remarks to his wife how early he gets to work and how great he is compared to his coworkers. His self-righteous actions were getting to work early for the wrong reasons (to judge others and remind himself how dedicated he is) and continually comparing himself to others.

When it comes to reconciling conflicts, people such as Bob, Sue, and Frank are in trouble from the get-go because they have skewed perspectives of who they are. They see themselves as better than they are and better than others. They also have a skewed perspective of God, seeing him as not really necessary to their lives. Such an attitude might result in something as insignificant as blaming a colleague for smelly exercise clothes when they really belong to you. But such an attitude might also lead to the loss of your marriage, cost you a job, or place a divide between you and your heavenly Father.

We need to be willing to see the logs in our lives and the specks in other people's lives. We live in a culture that teaches us that humility is not necessarily a virtue. We extol people who confidently march through life, even if they trample a few people along the way. But such priorities are not the priorities of a peacemaker (we'll discuss humility more fully in chap. 18). Peacemakers see themselves and others through God's perspective. They own their own baggage, even if God promises that they needn't stay shackled to it. And they look for the best in others instead of putting them down to bolster their own egos.

In real-life conflict, humility works wonders. Remember the story of the basketball coaches? A year later, the two teams played again. Before the game, the assistant coach of the Christian team came to the coach of the losing team as their teams were warming up. He extended a hand and introduced himself.

"Weren't you that coach who called us out last year for our behavior?" he asked.

The coach dropped his head, not particularly proud of that postgame moment. "Yeah, that was me," he said. "I'm sorry I got carried away after the game."

"Hey, we deserved it. We got carried away too. We lost perspective. We needed that admonition, even if we didn't act like it at the time."

The story didn't end there. A month later, the assistant coach invited the coach of the losing team to speak to the kids at the Christian school—not about this incident but about his job as a journalist in their community. The man accepted. During his speech, the coach did tell the story of the basketball game, honoring the assistant coach for having the guts, the courage, and the humility to recognize how he and the head coach had lost perspective. But in telling the story, he confessed that he too had lost perspective.

So a conflict that looked like it was going to tarnish the glory of God and maintain a wall between the coaches instead came to a peaceful resolution. A lose-lose-lose situation (coach 1, coach 2, and God's glory) became a win-win-win situation. Why? Because the assistant coach of the winning team faced the log in his own eye while recognizing only a speck in the other coach's eye. The losing coach, in response, did the same.

In God's economy, winning has nothing to do with a scoreboard and everything to do with our glorifying God through humbling ourselves to restore peace.

17

The Gospel

The same Gospel that saves you is the same Gospel that will keep you.

Author unknown

In a board meeting, I had just read 1 Corinthians 15:1–8, about the death and resurrection of Christ, when the Holy Spirit prompted me to ask the seven people in the room a question about me, their pastor.

"What," I said, "is something I need to die to as a leader?"

It's not the kind of question I ask every day; that probably explained a few of the perplexed looks on people's faces.

"I've been serving you for five years," I said. "What can I die to as a pastor?"

Nobody said a word. I walked to the whiteboard and wrote, "Death—Burial—Resurrection—Appearance." I recapped the pen and turned back to them.

"Seriously, I want to serve this church the best I can. What is something I need to die to?"

Each board member started sharing their own temptations, sins, and shortcomings. After half an hour of this, I asked again, "What about me? What do I need to die to?"

One board member cleared his throat. "Pastor, I think you overwork yourself because you think that if the church is going to succeed, it's up to you. You are, in essence, working every day because you don't trust that God can fill in the times you're not working. That's what I think you need to die to."

The room quieted again. I was genuinely appreciative of the admonishment. He was right. "Thank you. So how do I bury that overworking and lack of trust in God to handle the church?"

"I think you should repent and place your trust in God," said another board member.

I nodded. "Thanks. And what would newness of life look like in this area?"

"I know we are short-staffed, but I think you need to take at least one day off a week," said the board member who'd spoken first. "Rest. Enjoy your family."

"Thank you. And how would I show you—how would my life offer evidence—that I'm walking in this new trust in God?"

"We really want you to take Fridays off," said yet another board member. "This would serve as evidence for us that you're trusting God with the church and investing time with your family."

"Great. Thank you for this feedback. It's a deal."

A couple weeks later, I forgot to do something, and so I ran into the church on a Friday to get it done. A board member driving by saw my van and pulled in.

"What are you doing here, Brian? I thought you agreed to take Fridays off."

"I forgot," I said, without much confidence my words would pass as an excuse. I was right.

"Sorry, we had an agreement," he said. "You need to be more organized during the week, and you must take Fridays off."

He was right. I'd failed to follow through on a promise. If we're going to be peacemakers, if we're going to be people of spiritual substance, if we're going to be people of integrity when it comes to dealing with and working with others, we need to be people of the gospel, people of truth, people whose "yes means yes and no means no."

In that meeting, I'd asked for help. I'd been vulnerable. I'd empowered my board to help me take a log out of my eye. And yet when they'd done just that, when they'd shown me a blind spot and offered me a solution—a solution I'd promised to keep—I'd let them down. I'd offered to die to something in word, but I hadn't done it in deed.

Where did I need to go? To the gospel. In such soil grow the seeds of genuine reflection. Farmers know how this works: life comes from death. *The Soil and Health: A Study of Organic Agriculture* describes how the "principle of stability" dominates through an "ever-recurring cycle . . . constituted of the successive and repeated process of birth, growth, maturity, death, and decay. . . . Death supersedes life and life rises again from what is dead."[1]

---

1. Albert Howard, *The Soil and Health: A Study of Organic Agriculture*, Culture of the Land (1947; repr. Lexington: University of Kentucky Press, 2006), 18.

A seed dying in the ground gives newness of life. And so it is for people, the promise rooted in the gospel itself. Says 1 Corinthians 15:1–8:

> Now I would remind you, brothers, of the gospel I preached to you, which you received, in which you stand, and by which you are being saved, if you hold fast to the word I preached to you—unless you believed in vain.
>
> For I delivered to you as of first importance what I also received: that Christ died for our sins in accordance with the Scriptures, that he was buried, that he was raised on the third day in accordance with the Scriptures, and that he appeared to Cephas, then to the twelve. Then he appeared to more than five hundred brothers at one time, most of whom are still alive, though some have fallen asleep. Then he appeared to James, then to all the apostles. Last of all, as to one untimely born, he appeared also to me. (ESV)

Jesus's death brought life. And our dying to sin brings us the kind of life that can bring peace out of conflict. "And he said to all, 'If anyone would come after me, let him deny himself and take up his cross daily and follow me'" (Luke 9:23 ESV).

One of the greatest ways to reflect is to look through the gospel, the story of Christ's life, death, and resurrection in the first four books of the New Testament: Matthew, Mark, Luke, and John.

Have you heard the gospel preached to you? Have you received it? Do you stand on it? Have you been saved by it? Do you hold fast to it? Look at these questions closely. Examine, reflect, and then ask yourself what your answers might mean in how you resolve conflict with those in your family, in your workplace, in your school, or in your community.

According to Scripture, the most important truth is that Jesus died for our sins. Story over? No. The story is just beginning. Jesus died. Everything up to this point comprises the first part of the gospel. Then Jesus was buried.

What is the relationship between death and burial? Why do those actions go together? They go together because one is the evidence of the other. Burial is the evidence of death in most cases. But not in this case. Instead, Jesus was raised on the third day. He was resurrected. Not only that, but he appeared to people. Many people. What is the relationship between resurrection and appearance? Appearance is the evidence of resurrection. Jesus appeared to Cephas, to the twelve disciples, to five hundred people, to James, to the apostles, and to Paul.

And so the parts of the gospel look like this:

- gospel action 1: death
- gospel evidence 1: burial
- gospel action 2: resurrection
- gospel evidence 2: appearance

I encourage you to return to 1 Corinthians 15:1–8 and read it again. How, you may wonder, does this death, burial, resurrection, and appearance help us in our relationships? The gospel is what transforms our relationship with God and thus transforms our relationships with others. Jesus died for us. We have to be willing to die to self if we ever want to experience the fullness of the gospel and the fullness of relationships.

What does picking up our cross and following Jesus mean? It means to die to self, to bury the old person, to walk in the resurrection of the new person, and to show the transformation to others as evidence or appearance.

Every relationship you have will be transformed, every situation you encounter will be God honoring when you die to self, when you bury the old behaviors, the old thoughts, the old ways through repentance. Every relationship will change if you walk in the new person. Every relationship will be powerful if you show the transformation in your love and behavior toward others.

Sinking our roots deep in the nourishment of God yields healthy leaves, healthy relationships, as Jeremiah 17:7–8 says: "Blessed is the one who trusts in the LORD, whose confidence is in him. They will be like a tree planted by the water that sends out its roots by the stream. It does not fear when heat comes; its leaves are always green. It has no worries in a year of drought and never fails to bear fruit" (NIV).

Will we be perfect? No. Even when I asked my staff to help me die to self, my old ways still came back to haunt me. But we will see God with new eyes. We will see ourselves with new eyes. And we will see others with new eyes. Such a combination can't help but restore our relationships with others to the way God intended them to be.

So we've learned the gospel. We've reflected. We've asked God to search us and to teach us. Now let's talk about connecting with the other person.

PART 5
CONNECT

18

Practicing Humility

Humility and patience are the surest proofs of the increase of love.

John Wesley

The NFL wide receiver reaches above the defensive back's outstretched arms, grabs the ball in the end zone, and instantaneously makes sure his feet are in bounds. The referee thrusts his two hands skyward. Touchdown! The receiver pounds his chest, nods his head, and struts around while a handful of teammates, one acting as a photographer, gather to honor him with a group shot. The crowd cheers. You'd have thought he'd cured cancer or walked on Mars. Nope. He caught a football in the end zone. The player poses for the would-be photo as if to say, "Aren't I something?"

Humility is not highly prized in America. In fact, you could argue just the opposite is true. We cheer, honor, elect, follow on Twitter, and generally admire people who—let's just come right out and say it—are arrogant. Athletes. Movie stars. Politicians. We're so taken by their power and prestige that we not only overlook their ample egos but also applaud them.

Oh, there are exceptions. Some players, when scoring a touchdown, take a knee to prayerfully thank God. Some running backs are mindful enough to realize that they didn't make it into the end zone on their own and quickly thank their offensive linemen. Some movie stars and politicians downplay their accomplishments. But humility doesn't come easily for us. Author Philip Yancey, in his book *Soul Survivor*, writes about traveling overseas and how common it is to see an arrogance and insensitivity among Americans toward those in whatever country they're in. He says that our tourists "walk with a swagger."[1] But humility is necessary if we want to progress as effective peacemakers.

On our journey to peacemaking, here's the trail that has brought us here:

- Tension. It's a fact of life; we need to learn to respond to it in a healthy way.
- Story. Everyone has one; gaining perspective on others gives us clarity.
- Ascend. We need to rise to our heavenly Father's perspective and values. God is gracious and compassionate. He cares about our conflicts.
- Reflect. We need to examine our lives through the Father's eyes. Humble reflection prepares our hearts.

1. Philip Yancey, *Soul Survivor: How Thirteen Unlikely Mentors Helped My Faith Survive the Church* (New York: Doubleday, 2001), xvi.

As we shift to the final part of our peacemaking process—connect—the most important thing we need to understand is that humility is key. Arrogance not only won't help two people or two groups iron out their differences but also will make the situation worse. Arrogance represents adding-gas-to-fire stupidity.

When humility steps in, on the other hand, Jesus wins. When humility steps in, we act justly, love mercy, and walk humbly. Respectful communication demonstrates the gospel. We connect to the things of God, which, in turn, connects us with the people we're dealing with. This increases the chances that we'll connect to our goal of a peaceful outcome.

"Part of humility is taking responsibility for my sin and asking forgiveness even when it doesn't feel good," said Pastor Chip Ingram. "God wants to heal and restore your relationships, but it's not easy."[2]

Humility requires a Christ-based attitude, not a culture-based attitude. When that wide receiver scored his touchdown, the crowd exalted him for his efforts and, to some degree, for his ego-fueled end zone celebration. But in peacemaking efforts, God exalts us for our willingness to empty ourselves of ego and humble ourselves as bond-servants of Christ, as expressed in Philippians 2:5–9: "Have this attitude in yourselves which was also in Christ Jesus, who, although He existed in the form of God, did not regard equality with God a thing to be grasped, but emptied Himself, taking the form of a bond-servant, and being made in the likeness of men. Being found in appearance as a man,

2. Chip Ingram, "Why We Fight with Those We Love," *Living on the Edge with Chip Ingram* (blog), February 9, 2009, http://workshop.livingontheedge.org/read-blog/archive/2009/02/09/why-we-fight-with-those-we-love.

He humbled Himself by becoming obedient to the point of death, even death on a cross. For this reason also, God highly exalted Him."

Of course, emptying and humbling ourselves is easier said than done. Alone, we can't do this, but when we allow the Holy Spirit to work through us, we can.

An Example of Humility

Though I've let pride get the better of me plenty of times, let me share a case in which God worked wonders through me.

A particular school had just experienced two teen suicides. The school was spiraling down emotionally and struggling from all it had gone through. The school's environment was riddled with inconsistency and bullying, and the students started blaming one another for the suicides. Desperate for a way to restore peace in a school now in conflict, the superintendent called a prison chaplain he'd heard of. Me.

My peacemaking partner and I sat down with the superintendent.

"We don't know what to do," he said. "Our high school is falling apart from the inside out. My staff and I are frustrated. People are shutting down."

Knowing this was going to be an intense and difficult week, we began interviewing staff to see what their perspectives were regarding the problem. As the interviews continued, a pattern emerged: there was a clear inconsistency of rules among teachers. Some allowed students to listen to music on their phones; others did not. Some allowed teasing; others did not. So students went from room to room, having to adjust their behavior accordingly. And if they didn't—not surprising, given the inconsistencies—teacher-student clashes took place that affected the entire class.

After we gathered and analyzed the information, I met with the faculty to offer our assessment and recommendations. "Students need consistency of rules from class to class," I said.

A female teacher raised her hand to ask a question. She asked. I answered. Apparently, it wasn't a satisfactory answer because she stormed out of the room, slamming the door as she left. It wasn't an incident I could simply overlook or pretend others hadn't seen. There wasn't an elephant in the room; there was a dinosaur.

Somehow I finished my presentation and answered a few questions, and then I enlisted the help of another teacher to find the one who had left. When we walked into her room, I was aghast. It looked as if a tornado had spun through the room—in fact, was still spinning. She was slamming cupboards. She was throwing books. She turned and eyed me with a look that could kill.

"I hate men always telling me what to do!" she shouted.

She was fairly short, so I got down on my knees by a desk. She responded with a look of suspicion, as if to say, "What are you doing?"

"So," I said, "can you tell me more?"

She hesitated, again wary of whatever approach I was taking.

"Everywhere I go, men are telling me what to do. Now *you*. Your answer to my question was lame. You can't tell me how to run *my* class."

The off-loading continued for a few minutes. I remained on my knees and let her spew, careful not to interrupt.

"I'm listening," I said. "Is there more?"

Yes, it turned out. But gradually she moved closer to me. Then like an Old West cowboy whose six-shooter is out of ammo, she stopped firing.

All was quiet for a moment. Then I said four words that were clearly the work of the Holy Spirit. "Will you forgive me?"

Her face froze in puzzlement, as if nobody had ever said those words to her before.

"I hurt you," I continued, "and I need your forgiveness."

She took another step closer like a wounded animal, afraid that I might do what others—probably men—had likely done to her: hurt her.

"I . . . forgive . . . you," she said. "I'm so embarrassed about how I threw a fit."

She started crying and came closer. The other teacher watched in awe.

"Can I give you a hug?" she said.

I broke into a smile. "Sure."

After a brief hug, she backed away.

"I have never had a man ask me to forgive him."

By now the other teacher was crying too. But here's the deal: because I listened to the Holy Spirit's directive to humble myself and ask forgiveness, the teacher was able to drop her pride and listen to my objective assessment of the school. In the end, she not only heeded many of my recommendations but also became an advocate for positive change at the school.

Would that have happened had I turned to pride instead of humility? With justification—OK, *worldly* justification— I could have shouted her down in the meeting or dared her to come back when she started to leave. Going into her room, I could have said, "You know, your childish behavior is moving us away from, not closer to, getting the school back on its feet!" And when she lambasted me with her you-can't-tell-me-how-to-run-*my*-class line, I could have said, "I was hired to pinpoint problems in the school that others aren't seeing, and I'm staring at one of those problems right now, lady." But that would have reduced our chances to help restore the school, and the last comment might have earned me a snapped rubber band to my arm (a negative use of tension!). What made the difference was humility. In retrospect, I honestly believe the physical gesture of getting down on my knees was the game changer.

I am almost six feet tall, and the woman was perhaps five feet three. By getting down on my knees and leaning against a desk, by not just *telling* her I respected her but also *showing* her, she softened her heart and widened her perspective. The situation wasn't about me. And it wasn't about her. It was about helping a school get healthy again after two tragedies.

Three Truths about Humility

The incident reveals three truths about humility.

First, humility is not only about words but also about gestures, not only about statements but also about body language, not only about what the other person hears but also about what the other person sees. Jesus comes into town on a donkey. What does that say about him? Jesus washes the disciples' feet. What does that say about him? Jesus bears a cross up a hill and dies for our sin. What does that say about him? Humility often comes without words.

Second, humility involves giving up our rights—even if we are "right." I had every right to respond to the woman with the same treatment she'd given me. After all, the fact that no other teacher responded the way she did suggested this wasn't my problem but hers. But remember that line in Philippians: "Although He existed in the form of God, did not regard equality with God a thing to be grasped" (v. 6). Jesus had the authority to get on his high horse, but he chose not to. He had the right to demand honor, but he gave up that right. We need to do the same.

Third, humility is triggered by the reminder that everyone has a story. I hardly knew this woman, but it didn't take a rocket scientist to realize that her size made her feel looked down upon, not only from a physical standpoint but also from a relational standpoint. What's more, her anger suggested that she felt a glaring lack of respect from the world at large. In the classroom, when she referred to men always telling her what to do, it became clear that she'd been treated harshly by men in her life.

So instead of focusing on trying to win the battle, I focused on appreciating, respecting, and empathizing with her story. Once I did, I realized that even though her anger was aimed at me, it actually stemmed from a far deeper place in her story regarding her experiences with men. And I understood I could defuse the situation by showing her the one thing she longed for: respect.

Keeping Our Eyes on Jesus

When it comes to connecting, we need to keep our eye on the ball—our focus on a God-honoring solution. Proverbs

4:25–27 says, "Let your eyes look directly ahead and let your gaze be fixed straight in front of you. Watch the path of your feet and all your ways will be established. Do not turn to the right nor to the left; turn your foot from evil."

We need to know where we're going. We can't let our emotions—or the other person's emotions—knock us off the path to peace. We need to stay the course even when emotions get involved. Much of this is predicated on our willingness to act in a way that is beyond ourselves. We must set our gaze directly on Jesus Christ, the ultimate example of humility, as we already saw in Philippians 2. We must watch the paths of our feet. We must be steadfast in our convictions to connect. When we try to connect, if we don't fix our eyes on Jesus, we make the process difficult, if not impossible. Focusing on Jesus is everything.

There's a great teachable moment in the old basketball movie *Hoosiers*. One of the player's fathers is the town drunk. The player worries that his dad is going to show up at the game drunk and embarrass him, the team, and the school. The coach, played by Gene Hackman, needs the player to stay in the game, not to check out mentally. The coach looks the young man right in the eye and says, "Keep your head in the game. You got that?"

God is telling us the same thing. Hebrews 12:1–2 says, "Therefore, since we have so great a cloud of witnesses surrounding us, let us also lay aside every encumbrance and the sin which so easily entangles us, and let us run with endurance the race that is set before us, fixing our eyes on Jesus, the author and perfecter of faith, who for the joy set before Him endured the cross, despising the shame, and has sat down at the right hand of the throne of God."

Be Just, Don't Demand It

Often in conflict, we want justice for ourselves; that's understandable. Nobody likes to be wronged. However, if we want to be reconciled, we need to seek justice for the hurt we caused the other person. The question is, Would you rather be right or would you rather be reconciled? That's the very question I faced in the school incident. Was it worth it to win the battle (me proving to the woman that she was wrong and I was right) but lose the war (the school's quest to return again to a peaceful environment)? Justice is an amazing attribute of God. He is a just God. We may not be able to remain completely impartial, but we should always be willing to be fair and treat others with fairness. "Never look for justice," said Oswald Chambers, "but never cease to give it."[3] Jesus said it better: "Love your neighbor as yourself" (Matt. 22:39). That's justice, pure and simple. Loving, respecting, and honoring someone just as we'd want to be loved, respected, and honored.

Beyond shunning justice for ourselves, we should be merciful, or kind, to the other person. How do we do this? Above all, by listening, by serving the other person well. When we connect with the other person, our goal is not to change them. We can't change them. Our goal is to reflect the gospel—that light that God has shone on us through the mercy of the heavenly Father—with the hope that they will change on their own.

Do you see what made the difference in the school incident? It wasn't me changing the woman. It was me showing

3. Oswald Chambers, "Suffering Afflictions and Going the Second Mile," *My Utmost for His Highest*, July 14, https://utmost.org/suffering-afflictions-and-going-the-second-mile/.

her enough respect that she ultimately opened herself to the process of reconciliation. When that happened, she was willing to see what we saw: the school needed to standardize its expectations in every classroom.

The teacher changed her perspective. And as we shall see in the next chapter, listening to gain perspective is integral. We might say listening is to connecting what shells are to tacos. Without it, nothing stays together.

19

Learning to Listen

We do God's work for our brothers and sisters when we learn to listen to them.

Dietrich Bonhoeffer

Over coffee, Eric and Lance were catching up on each other's lives when Eric decided to heed the encouragement of his men's group at church and be vulnerable.

"So," he said, "Carol and I finally went in for counseling."

"Cool," said Lance, sipping a blended mocha. "What triggered that?"

"Oh, Carol says I don't listen to her."

"And is that true?"

"Beats me."

"Well, what did the counselor say? Did your counselor think that was a problem for you?"

"I don't know," said Eric. "I wasn't really paying much attention."

I'm going to go out on a limb here and suggest that Carol and Eric are going to have a hard time making progress in their marriage with this dynamic in play. It doesn't matter what the issue is, how desperately Carol wants revival for the marriage, or what Eric's perspective on the marriage might be. If either of the two parties involved isn't committed to listening to the other, the effort is doomed.

We can chuckle at Eric's disregard for paying attention, but the reality is that not listening to the other person short-circuits more attempts at reconciliation than anything else. Listening is the best gift we can give to someone in such a situation because it unlocks something that every success-ful peacemaking session requires: perspective. Each of the two parties must be willing to look at the situation not only through their own eyes but also through the eyes of the other.

"So often Christians, especially preachers, think that their only service is always to have to 'offer' something when they are together with other people," said Dietrich Bonhoeffer. "They forget that listening can be a greater service than speaking. Many people seek a sympathetic ear and do not find it among Christians, because these Christians are talking even when they should be listening."[1] James 1:19 says succinctly, "Everyone must be quick to hear, slow to speak and slow to anger."

It Takes Two

It takes two to resolve a conflict, and if we're not willing to consider another's point of view, why should we expect

1. Dietrich Bonhoeffer, *Life Together and Prayerbook of the Bible*, Dietrich Bonhoeffer Works, vol. 5, trans. by Daniel W. Bloesch and James H. Burtness (Minneapolis: Fortress Press, 2004), 98.

them to consider ours? Let me tell you of a recent interaction I had with a couple. They'd been fighting far beyond the fifteen-round limit.

"Tell me your stories from the beginning," I said.

He went first. For about an hour, he told me about his childhood. About his first marriage. About his current marriage and how the two fought about everything.

"I want to be her best friend," he said, "but nothing seems to work."

After he finished, there were a few moments of silence. I asked if he wanted to say more.

"No," he said. "I think that's it. Thanks for listening."

Then I turned to his spouse. She had been silent but polite. "OK, the goal here isn't to rebut what he just said," I said. "I just want you to tell me your story from the beginning."

She did so. She told me about a difficult childhood. About an abusive first husband, a nonbeliever. About how when she met her current husband, who was a Christian, she was anxious to have the kind of marriage she'd always hoped for.

"But once we got married, it was like a switch flipped. He started giving me the silent treatment for weeks. Oftentimes, I wouldn't even know what I'd done wrong." She went on for another ninety minutes, telling me all that was wrong with their marriage. She brought up incident after incident, hurt after hurt. When she was finished, I asked if either had any more to add. They did not.

"Great. What I'm going to do now is write down on individual sheets of paper everything I heard you say—one hurt per page."

The two nodded, though obviously they were a tad skeptical about where I was going with this. I took out a Sharpie and in big print wrote down each hurt I'd heard from each person. Page after page after page. On and on.

"This looking right?" I asked.

Both nodded. I added some more.

"Did I get them all?"

Both added a few more. Soon there were almost seventy sheets of paper filled with hurts, written in my sloppy handwriting. We started praying our way through each one.

What was noteworthy about the interaction was that this was the first time either of them had truly listened to the hurts of the other. At times, as we worked our way through the pages, one of them would add clarity. Or offer an apology. Or say something to the effect of, "I'm sorry, I'm just not ready to ask forgiveness for that one" or "I need more time." I left the session encouraged that they could make some headway in their marriage. Why? Because for the first time, instead of lobbing grenades at each other or giving each other the silent treatment, they were listening. They understood that finding peace wasn't about pointing fingers but about opening their ears, hearts, and minds to each other.

We often expect the other person to do this, but we should also expect it of ourselves. When we do this, we find that, yes, we've hurt the other person in some ways we didn't realize. The other person learns they have hurt us in some ways they didn't realize. But we also find what we've called shared perspective, things we both agree on. The couple I met with discovered the following:

- We both want to fight for our marriage.
- We both have made mistakes.
- We come from different backgrounds and must respect each other's differences.

Working Together

We may have lived for years or even decades with someone thinking we shared little in common. Sometimes listening to each other's struggles brings out the shared perspectives and works *for* the relationship instead of *against* it.

Connecting with someone moves us outside our own stories and into the other person's story.

As I mentioned in chapter 15, there are six perspectives to consider in each attempt at peacemaking: your perspective, the other person's perspective, the shared perspective created where the two perspectives overlap, God's perspective, the eternal perspective, and finally the new perspective created by considering all of these other perspectives.

Sometimes people fear discovering new information from the other person because it's hurtful: "I opened a separate checking account because I didn't trust you with our money." Ouch. But at least it's on the table and offers the potential for the two people to work through that problem, now that they know how far the roots of it go.

But discovering new information can also help restore a relationship that was thought dead. For example, in the prodigal son story, look at what the younger son knew: "The son said to him, 'Father, I have sinned against heaven and in your sight; I am no longer worthy to be called your son'" (Luke 15:21). What he knew wasn't particularly hopeful: "I messed up. I'm unworthy. You're likely ashamed of me. You likely want nothing to do with me, given how I squandered my inheritance."

But because he dared to initiate interaction with his father—that is, he dared to come home—look at what the younger son discovered: "But the father said to his slaves, 'Quickly bring out the best robe and put it on him, and put a ring on his hand and sandals on his feet; and bring the fattened calf, kill it, and let us eat and celebrate; for this son of mine was dead and has come to life again; he was lost and has been found.' And they began to celebrate" (15:22–24). What he discovered was hopeful beyond his wildest imagination: "Even though I screwed up, my father still loves me so much. In fact, he's honoring me upon my return."

When such reconciliation occurs, celebration is in order. How amazing when a relationship that once was lost is ultimately found.

20

A Path of a Peacemaker Conversation

The faith to step out is worthless without the faithfulness to stick it out.

Steven Furtick

During World War II, when the Allied forces stormed the beaches at Normandy in 1944 in an attempt—successful, as it turned out—to restore freedom to the world, the plans were intricate. They had to be. The invasion involved 326,547 troops, 54,186 vehicles, and 6,939 vessels. The tides needed to be just right. The weather needed to be just right. The timing of everything needed to be just right when the Air Force shelled the beaches to create holes in the sand (cover for the troops coming ashore), when the paratroopers had to drop at night behind enemy lines to take out German artillery installations, and when the landing crafts were to hit the beaches.

Not surprisingly, not everything went according to plan. Those shell holes, for example, weren't far enough up the beach, and as the incoming tide covered them, many soldiers sank in them as they splashed ashore with full equipment packs on their backs. But the overall effort was successful.

Keep that in mind when you set up, plan, and begin a connect session, or a path of a peacemaker conversation. It will likely not go just as you envision it. The other person may be reluctant to own their responsibility. They may sit with arms folded, meeting you only with great reluctance. You may accidentally stick your foot in your mouth. Don't panic. A path of a peacemaker conversation is not about perfection. It's about being willing. It's about being vulnerable. It's about being sincere in seeking peace. It's about caring enough to involve yourself in something that—let's face it—could be uncomfortable.

Pray. Be real. Be compassionate. Be mindful that this person is not your enemy, even if you have reason to believe they think so. All you can do is allow the Holy Spirit to work with you. You can't control the other person's response. Remember Romans 12:18: "So far as it depends on you, be at peace with all men." You can only do what you can or what God can do through you.

Initiating the New Normal

Someone has to initiate the new normal. In this case, a son dared to make contact with a father who had every reason

194

not to open the door. Instead, the father opened not only the door but also his arms to reconciliation.

Which raises the question, How do you invite someone into a peacemaking conversation? How do you initiate a connect session with a friend with whom you've developed a rift?

First, take the initiative. Scary? You bet. Despite the prodigal son's flaws, he came to his senses and went home. His father did not hunt him down and find him. Instead, the son returned to his father. He took the initiative even as he probably trembled in his sandals. The reason you're scared is because something has come between you and the other person, and you don't know how the other person will react. But remember this: if you take this step, there's at least a chance things will get better. If you don't, there's a good chance things will never get better. Are you willing to lose the relationship just because the first step might be painful?

"But they're the one who hurt *me*," you might say. "Why should I initiate this? It's their responsibility." And you might be 100 percent correct. On the other hand, they might be thinking the same thing regarding you, which leaves the relationship in a stalemate. Someone has to take the step. Be brave. Let it be you.

Second, own a part of the falling out, even if only a small part. "I was thinking about what happened between us. There are some things I could have and should have done better. I didn't live up to my convictions as a follower of Christ. Could we sit down and talk?" Or "I blew it when we were talking the other day. Can I buy you a cup of coffee so we can discuss what happened?"

Immediately, the person being asked into the conversation will let down their guard because they realize you aren't out to attack them. Now, some people with bad intentions might use this as a Trojan horse approach—make nice to get the other person's buy-in for a meeting then unload their blame gun once the session begins. Don't be one of those people.

Third, emphasize that you've reflected on the situation. "I've been praying about this . . ." or "I huddled with a pastor about this . . ." or simply "I've been giving this a lot of thought . . ." Such an approach shows you're not out for revenge or to vent; instead, you're honestly seeking a solution and want to be part of that solution.

Fourth, emphasize your willingness to listen. "I wonder if we can get together to talk about what happened. I'd like to hear your perspective."

Fifth, express your willingness to search your own heart instead of assuming the conflict was the other person's fault. "I sat down the other day and asked God to search me and teach me what I could have done better in our relationship. He showed me three things I need to ask your forgiveness for and commit to working on. Would you be willing to sit down and talk?"

What if, after searching your soul and praying about the situation, you honestly don't think you have anything to answer for? How, then, do you initiate a connect session? How about this: "I sensed tension between us. I would like you to help me see my blind spots. Do you have time to talk?" The overall thrust here says a couple things to the other person: first, you truly care about the relationship; second, you're willing to consider that you might be part of the problem.

Conversely, what if you're fairly certain that you blew it big time, that you might, in fact, be responsible for the relationship going south? Just be up front: "Hey, I care about you deeply, but I can be a jerk at times. What happened at the gym the other day was an example of that tendency. I'm sorry. Can we get together to talk about it?"

In family settings, the initiation might be slightly different. For example, a husband might say to his wife, "I know I'm supposed to be a leader in our family. I don't feel like I've done a good job of demonstrating humility, gentleness, and kindness. Can we talk about it?" Again, this disarms the wife because the husband is admitting some of his shortcomings.

Don't beat around the bush, however. If there's hurt in the relationship, say it. "I sense there's a wall between us," a wife might say. "I was reflecting on what I could do to make that better. Can we take a walk and talk about it?"

A father might go to a child who is ten years old or older with a line like this: "I want to talk about how I can be a better dad for you. I know we got in an argument last night. Let's talk."

Finally, there's that in-your-dreams moment when your teenager says, "Mom (or Dad), can we talk? I was rude last night in our conversation." (As I said, you can always dream!)

Regardless of the situation and regardless of who it involves, an invitation to what I call a path of a peacemaker conversation looks like this:

humility +	acknowledging reflection	+ asking =	an invitation to a path of a peacemaker conversation

Starting a Conversation

Let me offer some examples of how a conversation might get started. Depending on the context, you might start your meeting with prayer; that's a great way to start. Prayer gives each person the broader perspective that this isn't about only two people and that the two of you aren't alone in working this out.

I'm going to use Bob and Sally in several examples to show how to start a path of a peacemaker conversation.

Business Example (Bob is Sally's boss)

BOB. Thanks for meeting with me. Is this still a good time to discuss what happened last week? As I said on the phone yesterday, after our discussion the other day, I was reflecting and feel I was rude and harsh to you.

SALLY. OK.

BOB. Would you be willing to share what happened from your perspective so that I can fully apologize?

SALLY. OK, last week when you yelled at me, it was a horrible day for me because . . .

Business Example (Sally is Bob's boss)

SALLY. Thanks for meeting with me. I feel like yesterday in the staff meeting our conversation didn't go so well.

BOB. OK.

SALLY. I'd like to ask you to share what happened from your perspective.

BOB. No, everything's cool. Not a big deal.

SALLY. Bob, we need to have a healthy relationship. It's important to me to hear your side of the story. Please share your perspective.

Church Example (Bob is the senior pastor, and Sally is the worship director)

BOB. Sally, thanks for meeting with me. Can we pray?

SALLY. Sure.

BOB. Lord, Sally and I acknowledge that you are here. Help us to see more clearly the problem and the solution. In Jesus's name, amen. Sally, I was harsh with you at our staff meeting the other day. Will you share what happened from your perspective?

SALLY. You threatened to fire me. I'm not sure I want to share.

BOB. I was wrong when I said that, and I apologize. Would it make you feel more comfortable to have a board member or an elder with us for this conversation?

SALLY. Actually, it would.

BOB. Let's reschedule. Which elder or board member would you like to be present?

SALLY. How about Phil Roberts?

BOB. Great. Do you want me to contact him or would you like to?

SALLY. I will.

BOB. Thank you. Again, our relationship is important. I'm asking God to search me and teach me how to be a better pastor. I look forward to our conversation.

The Parts of a Conversation

The key to starting a path of a peacemaker conversation is, as I've said before, humility. Sometimes you'll need to set the tone at the beginning of the conversation by confessing what the Holy Spirit revealed to you during reflection. Remember, you want to hear the other person's story. The key to listening is that you don't try to rebut the other person. They are explaining the tension from their perspective. Let them share.

Many people ask, "Do I share my story after they share their story?" That depends on how the conversation goes. The process—story, ascend, reflect, and connect—does not necessarily unfold in a linear fashion. You may listen to their story and then reflect. Then you may jump back to storytelling, ascend, followed by more reflection. Everything depends on the situation. Let the Holy Spirit lead.

Now let's go deeper into an example involving Bob and Sally, a married couple. Bob has invited Sally to talk by saying, "I know I'm supposed to be a leader in our family, but I don't feel like I've done a good job of demonstrating humility, gentleness, and kindness. May we get coffee to talk about it?" Here is how their conversation may play out.

 Story

BOB. Honey, I was rude to you last night. Will you tell me how I hurt you?

SALLY. Yes, you were rude.

Sally explains that he hurt her by bringing up past hurts.

200

⌓ Ascend

BOB. I'm sorry I hurt you. Can we pray? Lord, I hurt my wife. I ask that you'll guide this conversation. Open my eyes, search my soul, and help me understand how I can be a better husband.

✐ Reflect

BOB. I was completely rude and had no right to bring up the past hurts.

SALLY. Do you now forgive me for those things?

BOB. I do. I don't know why I said what I did. I'm sorry.

↪ Connect

BOB. I broke relationship with you when I was rude. Will you forgive me?

SALLY. I need some time to process this because this seems to be a pattern, and it's hurtful. It makes me feel worthless, like I can't do anything right.

BOB. I understand. How, specifically, can I love you better as a husband?

SALLY. I think you could . . .

Sally offers a handful of suggestions.

Do you see how we move from ascend to taking personal responsibility? It's subtle and, again, it probably will not be this linear. In connect, Bob not only reaffirms how sorry he is but also makes a commitment to do better in the future. He asks for specific ways he hurt Sally, which gives her the opportunity to deepen her story.

The primary parts of connect are to ask, confess, seek, and forgive. What exactly does this look like? You're about to find out. Like buying a high-risk stock, being all in takes some courage, but the dividends are out of this world, literally, because only the Holy Spirit can change hearts like this.

21

Forgiveness

Forgiveness is not that stripe which says, "I will forgive, but not forget." It is not to bury the hatchet with the handle sticking out of the ground, so you can grasp it the minute you want it.

Dwight L. Moody

I sat down with a couple from Texas. The man had been a children's pastor for twenty years. The week before, his wife had caught him looking at pornography on the family computer. She had gone to the elders of the church for help and accountability. First, they removed him as the church's children's pastor. In their church, he was required to confess the sin to the entire church body. The elders had asked me to help him write his confession.

This was an emotional time for everyone, especially for the couple. It was heart-wrenching. I looked the man in the eye.

"How has your sin hurt others?"

He didn't flinch. "I don't think it has hurt others at all. It is and was a private sin. I was hurting only myself."

"Mind if we ask your wife?"

I turned to her.

"How has your husband's sin hurt you?"

Her answer came with a floodgate of tears. "I'm embarrassed to live in our community. I'm embarrassed to have your last name. I feel like everyone stares at me at the grocery store. The kids—*our* kids—don't want to go to school out of embarrassment. I lost my security because you are not a pastor anymore." She was just getting started. "For twenty years I thought we had a great marriage, but now I realize I got only half of your love. The other half went to your computer and yourself."

I turned to him and looked him in the eye again. He sat quietly. Then tears started running down his face, and he began to sob. He fell onto his knees. He finally realized how his sin had hurt others. He finally realized how he had justified it for years as private and hurting only himself. He finally realized that he had stolen love that was supposed to be his wife's.

He owned his sin. The following Sunday he went before his church and took responsibility for his actions. He was forthright. He was genuine. He was clearly touched by the Holy Spirit. The congregation saw it and embraced him.

Then the hard work began. He faced several years of rehab. He would never be employed at that church again. But I'm proud to say that, years later, he is back in ministry and porn-free. Meanwhile, bit by bit, he won back the respect of his family, the church, and the community.

Why? Because he had the courage to take responsibility and ask for forgiveness.

Psalm 32 says it all about confession, forgiveness, and God's response. While this Psalm of David explores his confession of sin to God, it is full of application for all our relationships.

> How blessed is he whose transgression is forgiven,
> Whose sin is covered!
> How blessed is the man to whom the LORD does not
>   impute iniquity,
> And in whose spirit there is no deceit!
>
> When I kept silent about my sin, my body wasted
>   away
> Through my groaning all day long.
> For day and night Your hand was heavy upon me;
> My vitality was drained away as with the fever heat
>   of summer.
> I acknowledged my sin to You,
> And my iniquity I did not hide;
> I said, "I will confess my transgressions to the
>   LORD";
> And You forgave the guilt of my sin.
> Therefore, let everyone who is godly pray to You in a
>   time when You may be found;
> Surely in a flood of great waters they will not reach
>   him.
> You are my hiding place; You preserve me from
>   trouble;
> You surround me with songs of deliverance.
>
> I will instruct you and teach you in the way which
>   you should go;
> I will counsel you with My eye upon you.
> Do not be as the horse or as the mule which have no
>   understanding,

Whose trappings include bit and bridle to hold them
  in check,
Otherwise they will not come near to you.
Many are the sorrows of the wicked,
But he who trusts in the LORD, lovingkindness shall
  surround him.
Be glad in the LORD and rejoice, you righteous
  ones;
And shout for joy, all you who are upright in heart.

A Breakdown of Psalm 32

*"How blessed is he whose transgression is forgiven, whose sin
is covered!" (v. 1).*

Two thousand years ago, Jesus covered all our sin. We
need to remind ourselves daily of this truth and that
we are blessed. Asking for forgiveness is less about our
words and more about what God has done through his
Son Jesus.

*"How blessed is the man to whom the LORD does not impute
iniquity, and in whose spirit there is no deceit!" (v. 2).*

This is why we ask God to search us. We want him to show
us the blind spots of our lives. We need honesty on the
inside and on the outside. Knowing that God has searched
or is searching us is a freeing experience.

*"When I kept silent about my sin, my body wasted away through
my groaning all day long" (v. 3).*

Sometimes we try to stay silent about our sin. We try,
but our hearts groan. God desires authentic worship. He
wants us to know silence is not an option. We can reach

out to God because he loves us. We need to let him reveal to us all that he wants to do in our lives.

"For day and night Your hand was heavy upon me; my vitality was drained away as with the fever heat of summer" (v. 4).

We must not lose heart. God's hand is heavy upon us because he cares for us. He desires the best for us. He wants to bring out the best in us.

"I acknowledged my sin to You, and my iniquity I did not hide; I said, 'I will confess my transgressions to the Lord'; and You forgave the guilt of my sin" (v. 5).

God is awesome. As we confess, as we release our broken relationships to him, he forgives. He brings peace. He removes the guilt.

"Therefore, let everyone who is godly pray to You in a time when You may be found; surely in a flood of great waters they will not reach him" (v. 6).

We need to take the time to pray to God, to seek out God. This is the time he can be found. God is our Protector.

"You are my hiding place; You preserve me from trouble; You surround me with songs of deliverance" (v. 7).

We don't often think of God singing songs of deliverance over us, but he does, even with all the multitudes of people in the world. He is God, and though we see singularly, God sees and sings with "multiple" vision.

"I will instruct you and teach you in the way which you should go; I will counsel you with My eye upon you" (v. 8).

What an amazing thought that the King of the universe sees us, instructs us, and teaches us.

"Do not be as the horse or as the mule which have no understanding, whose trappings include bit and bridle to hold them in check, otherwise they will not come near to you" (v. 9).
We must not be impulsive like a horse or stubborn like a mule. We must be teachable before God. We must let him instruct us freely so he doesn't have to instruct us through control.

"Many are the sorrows of the wicked, but he who trusts in the LORD, lovingkindness shall surround him" (v. 10).
When we trust in the Lord, he will surround us with lovingkindness. We can trust God in the good times and in the hard times.

"Be glad in the LORD and rejoice, you righteous ones; and shout for joy, all you who are upright in heart" (v. 11).
This is a time to be glad and to rejoice as we confess our sin to God, for he makes us righteous. Even so, as with the case of the children's pastor, oftentimes we must take additional steps to secure forgiveness from those whom our sin has affected.

The Process of Connecting

In the New Testament, Colossians 3:12–13 says, "So, as those who have been chosen of God, holy and beloved, put on a heart of compassion, kindness, humility, gentleness and patience; bearing with one another, and forgiving each other, whoever has a complaint against anyone; just as the Lord forgave you, so also should you."

While connecting with others, we have the opportunity to have a heart of compassion, to forgive, to show the other person kindness, humility, gentleness, and patience. We're to do this in the same way that Jesus does. Jesus forgives us completely. Jesus is 100 percent kind and humble, gentle and patient. As we prepare to meet for a path of a peacemaker conversation with someone, we should prayerfully consider what percentage of forgiveness, kindness, humility, gentleness, and patience we're willing to show to the other person. (Hint: The right answer is 100 percent. As Jesus shows to us, we should show to others.)

Connecting moves us to a new perspective and hopefully to a new story of grace, mercy, and forgiveness—a gospel story. The four-step process is to ask, confess, seek, and forgive.

Ask

One of the best ways to connect with the other person or group is to ask a question. For example:

- What impact have my actions had on you?
- How have I hurt you?
- What do you believe the consequences of my actions should be?
- What are some of my blind spots?
- How would you like me to change?
- How have I sinned against you?
- What are some things I need to sacrifice, give up, die to?
- How can I better serve you?

- How can I be a better spouse?
- How have I treated you unfairly?
- How can I better see your perspective?
- Is there anything I could have done better?
- How have I hurt our relationship?
- How can I grow?
- How can I be a better employee?
- How can I be a better boss or manager?
- What are five things I can do to serve you better?

Confess

After we have asked and the other person has answered, we begin to confess our sin to them. Sometimes we may not agree with their assessment, or we may want to justify our motives. We need to be careful not to do this during our confession. We especially need to avoid the following statements.

"You" statements. "You did . . ." "You hurt me by . . ." You statements are not confessions. You statements are accusations. We should use "I" statements instead: "I was rude," "I was mean," "I gossiped," "I tore you down," "I was anxious," "I did not speak up."

"But" statements. These statements negate whatever statement preceded them. "I did this, but you did that"; "I ask for your forgiveness, but why am I always the one apologizing?" But statements cancel any progress made with I statements. We should flee from them.

Self-justifying statements. These are close-but-no-cigar statements in which we confess to acting badly but with the caveat that there was a good reason for it. "I was wrong to be rude to you, but I was having a really bad day"; "I apologize for ignoring your needs, but it's not as if I don't have a few unmet needs of my own." Offering context helps, but confession is not the appropriate time to do so.

"If" statements. These statements suggest we didn't do the wrong we did. "I'm sorry if I hurt you"; "If you think I acted inappropriately, then let's talk about it." The hidden message is "I don't really think I hurt you, and so I don't think I should have to apologize, but if it will help calm the storm . . ." If you're unsure whether you hurt someone, ask them. If you do know you hurt someone, say so.

"Maybe" and "might have" statements. These are useless as well. "I might have hurt you when I . . ." "Maybe next time I will . . ." This kind of tiptoeing doesn't do anyone any good. We need to make solid statements and own our behavior.

Here are some confession statements:

- I admit I . . .
- I hurt you when I . . .
- I understand _____ is the consequence.
- Next time I will . . .
- My accountability plan is . . .
- My restitution plan is . . .
- I was wrong when I . . .
- I sinned against you when I . . .

- I hurt our relationship when I . . .
- I broke our trust by . . .

Seek

Now we get the opportunity to seek forgiveness. This is the gospel in all its fullness. This is acknowledging we have treated the other person unjustly, with a lack of mercy, or without humility.

- Will you forgive me for . . . ?
- Are you able to forgive me for . . . ?
- Do you need time to consider my request?

While teaching workshops, I've come to realize that this step can be difficult for people, particularly if they think the other person has some forgiveness seeking of their own to do. A part of this step is choosing to do the following with God's help.

By God's empowering grace:

- I choose to entrust my pain to God.
- I choose to give up my desire for revenge.
- I choose to let go of all bitterness and resentment.
- I choose to offer a gift of grace.

Forgive

The final step is one that is out of our hands. The other person needs to forgive. But it is also important to recognize that at other times, we will be the one who needs to forgive. How do we release supernatural forgiveness? The answer is in

Ephesians 4:32: "Be kind to one another, tender-hearted, for-giving each other, just as God in Christ also has forgiven you."
We love because God first loved us. We forgive because God first forgave us. How do we forgive as God forgives? Let's use Joseph as an example.

> Forgiveness is confidential. When Joseph was going to confront his brothers, he said, "Have everyone go out from me" (Gen. 45:1). We forgive by keeping others' offenses confidential. If I said I forgive you but I posted what you did on Facebook, would you really believe I forgave you? The story I shared earlier about the children's pastor is slightly different. The pastor's public confession was a consequence for that particular church. The confidentiality I am talking about here has to do with avoiding gossip and slander.
>
> Forgiveness draws the offender closer. "Please come closer to me," Joseph said to his brothers (Gen. 45:4). Typically, when we're mad at someone, the last thing we want to do is invite them closer to us. But if we want to forgive as God forgives, we need to open our hearts and invite the other person into dialogue. There are, of course, special situations when abuse has taken place and drawing the offender closer wouldn't be appropriate; I'm not suggesting you place yourself in harm's way. In such situations, outside help is necessary. In normal, nonabusive relationships, however, we must be willing to draw the other person into right relationship.
>
> Forgiveness is honest but wants the best for the offender. Joseph told his brothers, "Now do not be grieved or

angry with yourselves, because you sold me here"
(Gen. 45:5). When we forgive, we do not sugarcoat
what happened, but we do not seek forgiveness-plus
either—that is, forgiveness plus revenge or forgiveness plus retribution or forgiveness plus anything
else. We seek forgiveness alone.

Forgiveness sees God's sovereignty and goodness in the
middle of conflict. Joseph said three times, "God sent
me" (Gen. 45:5, 7–8). This is incredibly difficult to
do in our own strength. We must ascend back to the
Father in order to do this.

Forgiveness protects the other person's reputation.
Then Joseph said, "Go up to my father, and say to
him, . . . 'God has made me lord of all Egypt'" (Gen.
45:9). Joseph could have easily said, "Go tell Dad
what you did." But he didn't. He in essence protected
his brothers' reputations. Joseph's father was smart
enough to come up with the proper conclusions on
his own. Joseph allowed for that, and he saw God's
hand at work in all of it.

Forgiveness transcends time and reoffense. Finally, after
Jacob had died and Joseph's brothers feared what
Joseph might do to them in their father's absence,
Joseph said, "Do not be afraid, for am I in God's
place?" (Gen. 50:19). Joseph was willing to forgive
even when his brothers reoffended. He maintained
forgiveness over a long period of time.

In short, we need to forgive others as God forgives us.
When we realize how forgiving God is—when we think of all
our sin that he's washed clean—we realize how much he loves

us and how love does not come easily. If we think forgiveness is hard—and it is—we must remember what he's done for us. Isaiah 1:18 says, "'Come now, let us settle the matter,' says the LORD. 'Though your sins are like scarlet, they shall be as white as snow; though they are red as crimson, they shall be like wool'" (NIV).

Let's close part 5 with a story that always reminds me that connecting is doable. A man just found out that his wife had $30,000 in debt on a credit card that he didn't know about. Thirty thousand dollars! And this was not a family rolling in dough.

The man was crushed. I looked him in the eye and said, "How long do you want to be angry, mad, bitter, and frustrated?"

He looked at me, perplexed.

"How long do you want to be angry, mad, bitter, and frustrated?" I repeated.

He thought it over.

"Two weeks."

"OK, let's talk in two weeks."

"Wait," he said. "Can I really put a time frame on my anger?"

"Sure," I said. "God does."

"He does?"

"Yeah, the Word says God's anger is for a moment, but his lovingkindness is for a lifetime. God's Word says, 'Do not let the sun go down on your anger.' Those are both time frames."

The man nodded his head. "OK."

In two weeks, I saw him. "Time's up," I said.

"I'm not ready yet," he said.

"Ready for what?"

"Ready to be over my anger."

"Too bad. You had your time. I gave you more time than I give most people. Today, I'm going to invite you to pray and release your anger to God. Then I'd like you to go and tell your wife you forgive her. Then every day from this day forward, as you're paying off that credit card bill, when bitterness tries to creep in, I want you to remember and say, 'On this day I forgave and released my wife.'"

He needed no persuading. Right there he prayed and released his anger to God. He immediately went to his wife and sat down beside her. "Right now, right here, I release my anger over the credit card to God," he said. "And I forgive you."

Her eyes grew wet. "Really?"

"Yes, really."

Although they are still paying off that debt, they are holding hands and laughing and kissing and being the couple God intended them to be. That is what forgiveness can do.

PART 6
CONCLUSION

22

What If Things Don't Go as You Hope?

It's hard to steer a parked car.

Jim Elliot

There are times when our peacemaking efforts don't seem to be going the way we wish. But before we resolve that we've hit a wall we can't go past, we can act. Our actions can speak louder than the words we say.

An Appeal for Action

The story was reflected in his tears, which slid down his face as if to suggest defeat. John shook his head in frustration.

"I have told my wife so many times that I'm sorry and that I will improve, but each and every time we get into a fight, I get rude and obnoxious," he said. "I really don't know what to do. She doesn't believe me anymore."

I looked at him. I hurt for him. I've seen plenty like him, one who occasionally stares back at me in the mirror.

"John, here's what I want you to do," I said. "Instead of *telling* her something, I want you to start *showing* her something, *doing* something."

"What do you mean?"

"Instead of telling her you're sorry, I want you to begin incorporating the 'one another' principles of Scripture into your relationship with her."

He said, "OK," but the word was tinted with a touch of skepticism. He wasn't unwilling to go there; he just wasn't sure where there was.

"John," I said, "love is a verb. It's about action. Sure, you can tell someone you love them, but what means more, saying 'I love you' or making a sacrifice for someone? Which would have meant more, Jesus saying he loved us or Jesus giving his life for us?"

I reached for my Bible and started offering examples of love as something we do, not just something we say.

- Greet one another (Rom. 16:16).
- Be kind to one another (Eph. 4:32).
- Forgive one another (Eph. 4:32).
- Show hospitality to one another (1 Pet. 4:9).
- Serve one another (Gal. 5:13).
- Submit to one another (Eph. 5:21).
- Comfort one another (1 Thess. 4:18).
- Bear with one another (Eph. 4:2).

- Encourage one another (1 Thess. 5:11).
- Build up one another (1 Thess. 5:11).
- Outdo one another in showing honor (Rom. 12:10).
- Stir up one another to love and good works (Heb. 10:24).
- Pray for one another (James 5:16).

"Do you see what I'm saying?"

"Yeah, I do."

"So here's your assignment. Instead of saying you're sorry and promising her you'll do better, take action. Every day I want you to pick one of these action steps and implement it. Choose, say, 'submit to one another' and yield to one another in love. Enough with the words, John. It's time for action."

My suggestion worked. John realized that love is more than words. Over time—and not without a few hiccups along the way—John and his wife became a couple again instead of two strangers fighting with each other.

Even though this book is based on a set of steps to help you find peace with someone you've been warring with, it's not about the process. The process is just a means to an end. What really matters is *action*. When you invite someone to sit and talk about something that has hurt you, that's taking action. When you forgive someone who's hurt you, that's taking action. When you make amends for some offense, that's taking action.

What If They Never Change?

But what if you go through the peacemaker process and it doesn't work? What if someone is simply unwilling to forgive, storms out of the session, or retaliates with a list of things you've done to hurt them?

In a perfect world, none of this would happen. But that perfect world is called heaven, and down here, we just get an occasional glimpse. So, yeah, things will go wrong. People won't always react as you'd like them to. The process will occasionally run off the tracks, crash into the woods, and explode into flames.

You can't expect perfect results with anything involving imperfect people. You can pray. You can get your heart right with God. You can listen for the Holy Spirit's promptings. You can make every attempt you can, sticking to scriptural guidelines, to help bring about reconciliation. But here's the thing: you aren't responsible for the results. You can't be. Why? Because as I've said many times, you can't control other people.

But here's what you *can* do: refuse to repay evil for evil.

Let me illustrate. Kathy tried to reconcile with her husband, but every time she did, her husband would yell, curse, and run out the door. He would be gone for hours, and she wouldn't know what to do. She was embarrassed by his behavior. The conflict spilled over into outbreaks that happened in public, at company parties, and at church. Everyone knew they were struggling.

She sat down and told me the story. She was looking for an easy answer.

"What if he never changes?" I said. "What then? What will you do?"

She looked at me, perplexed.

"What if, from now until the day he dies, he is the same way?"

"I don't know if I can take it. I mean, I want to be happy."

"Will you have more days with your husband broken and sinful or more days with him whole and complete in heaven?"

She had never thought of it that way.

"Is he abusing you? Is he hitting you or calling you names or threatening you?" (If this was the case, she would need to get out of that situation immediately.)

"No, he's just like a little baby throwing temper tantrums. It is just very embarrassing."

"Marriage," I said, "is like the gospel."

"What do you mean?"

I opened the Bible to Romans 5:6–11 and read:

For while we were still weak, at the right time Christ died for the ungodly. For one will scarcely die for a righteous person—though perhaps for a good person one would dare even to die—but God shows his love for us in that while we were still sinners, Christ died for us. Since, therefore, we have now been justified by his blood, much more shall we be saved by him from the wrath of God. For if while we were enemies we were reconciled to God by the death of his Son, much more, now that we are reconciled, shall we be saved by his life. More than that, we also rejoice in God through our Lord Jesus Christ, through whom we have now received reconciliation. (ESV)

"Right now," I said, "your husband is like an enemy to you."

"Well, that might be a little strong. He's more like a pain in the neck."

"OK, he's a pain in the neck. What did Christ do when we were all pains in his neck?"

Her brows furrowed in doubt. "Wait, are you saying I should just let him be embarrassing and obnoxious?"

"I'm saying, 'How might you show the work of the gospel in your heart?'"

"I don't know. That's why I'm here."

"What if we prayed this week for God to show you how you might reflect the gospel to your husband?"

"It's worth a try, I guess."

In a quick-fix world, the reality is that the peacemaking process takes time, patience, courage, and above all, faith. At times, things will go awry. For example, you might get to the part of the process where you're expecting the other party to ascend—identify with the things of God. Instead, the person descends—identifies with self. As you might recall, that is what the older brother did in the prodigal son story. Luke 15:25–32 says:

> Now his older son was in the field, and when he came and approached the house, he heard music and dancing. And he summoned one of the servants and began inquiring what these things could be. And he said to him, "Your brother has come, and your father has killed the fattened calf because he has received him back safe and sound." But he became angry and was not willing to go in; and his father came out and began pleading with him. But he answered and said to his father, "Look! For so many years I have been serving you and I have never neglected a command of yours; and yet you have never given me a young goat, so that I might celebrate with my friends; but when this son of yours came, who has devoured your wealth with prostitutes, you killed the fattened calf for him." And he said to him, "Son, you have always been with me, and all that is mine is yours. But we had

to celebrate and rejoice, for this brother of yours was dead and has begun to live, and was lost and has been found."

And what if *you* descend? What if *you* start yelling? What if *you* start breaking relationship with the other person? What if *you* lose it?

God calls peacemakers to be pursuers. "If possible, so far as it depends on you, be at peace with all men" (Rom. 12:18). What that doesn't mean is that when you make your overture to the other person, things are going to magically change.

At the church he attended, a friend of mine acted based on unrealistic expectations after the resignation of a pastor and a close friend of his. My friend believed the pastor had, at worst, been forced out and, at best, been killed by neglect by a board that had underestimated how valuable he was. He wrote an impassioned letter pointing out to the board the error of their ways and, at a meeting, encouraged them to read it. They didn't move a bit from their position.

"The lesson for me," he told me later, "was that we don't always get what we want. But seeking peace and justice is still the right thing to do. We act in obedience to the Lord, but the chips fall where they may. We don't orchestrate the end result; we can't, even if we so often would like to. Our job is to be faithful to the desires of the Lord."

A Second Look: We All Have Blind Spots

Once you have heard and understood the other person's story, you may want to revisit your own story and your own conclusions, because "all the ways of a man are clean in his own sight, but the LORD weighs the motives" (Prov. 16:2).

When detectives have done their research but still can't figure out who committed a crime, what do they do? They go back and rethink every clue, every action, every motivation. In your case, you're not looking for the perpetrator of a crime; you're looking for a pathway to peace and what will get you there. As part of that review, you might need to weigh your motives and ask the following second-look questions:

- What did I miss?
- What wasn't I aware of previously?
- What do I still think I'm right about?
- What new tensions did I discover?
- How did my understanding of my possible contribution to the conflict change?
- What did I discover about my words or actions that created a loss in the other person's life?
- Did the other person cause me any losses that I wasn't previously aware of, and have I grieved those losses? If I have, am I willing to forgive that person?
- If I caused losses in the life of the other person, am I willing to be responsible for the damage I caused?
- Now that I've heard the other person's side of the story, can we resolve the problem the way I originally thought? If not, what needs to change in my original idea to address what is important to the other person?

What else can you do during a second look? Instead of wrapping yourself up in your own feelings, ascend to God's perspective: "Be kind to one another, tender-hearted, forgiving each other, just as God in Christ also has forgiven you" (Eph. 4:32). Consider the amazing truth "that, in reference to your former manner of life, you lay aside the old self, which is being corrupted in accordance with the lusts of deceit, and that you be renewed in the spirit of your mind, and put on the new self, which in the likeness of God has been created in righteousness and holiness of the truth" (Eph. 4:22–24).

Your prayer might be this: "Lord, I need to die to unforgiveness. I'm wrong to carry this stuff. I repent. I turn. Thank you for empowering me to forgive the way Jesus forgives." Or this: "Lord, Charlie won't forgive me, and that hurts. But I take my pain and my hurt, and I lay them down at the cross. Lord, help me to love Charlie in a way I can't on my own. Help me to show the kind of forgiveness that will bring you glory." Finally, you might then return to the connect step. "Here are five ways I'm going to show Charlie forgiveness."

23

Go in Peace

Optimism is the faith that leads to achievement. Nothing can be done without hope and confidence.

Helen Keller

The wildfire was burning, and Joe, a pastor for twenty years, needed to put it out. A couple who had been attending his church for ten years—in other words, a couple who should have known better—had been talking behind his back. Undermining him. Throwing more brush on the burn pile.

"Brian, God is calling me to talk to them," he told me.

"And what's the issue?"

"Bottom line—they don't like my leadership."

"What's accurate about what they are saying?"

Joe recoiled a touch. "Excuse me?"

"I'm sure you can see what's *inaccurate* about what they're saying," I said, "but what is *accurate*?"

"Hmm. They say I'm pushy and demanding, which I suppose I can be from time to time. I really struggle with that."

"OK, start there. Invite them to the conversation by saying something like, 'I know I can be demanding at times. Would you be willing to sit down and talk about this with me?'"

"Really?"

"Really," I said.

"Then what?"

"When you sit down, pray, and then ask them to tell you what's going on from their perspective."

"But I really don't want to talk about me," he said. "I want to talk about them slandering me to the church."

"OK, but what does Jesus say about the log?"

He didn't want to answer that one, but he knew his Scripture.

"Take it out of your eye first."

"Then you will see clearly to take the speck out of their eye."

"But what if they don't bring up their speck?"

"Then you can bring it up, but I can almost guarantee they will begin to talk about it. Meanwhile, don't concentrate on their speck; let God worry about that. Concentrate on the log in your eye."

We prayed that he'd have courage and good perspective regarding the whole log-speck thing. A few weeks later after he'd met with them, we talked again.

The meeting had exceeded his expectations. The couple forgave his demanding nature and asked for forgiveness for slandering him. What's more, he learned a little something about himself through the process. He learned he *did* push people too hard.

I was proud of him for pursuing peace. "Beginning well is a momentary thing," said Ravi Zacharias. "Finishing well is a lifelong thing."[1]

Walk the Talk

Joe's case was pretty simple. As you might expect, not all are that cut-and-dried. Had there been friction in his first discussion with the couple, Joe might have benefited from taking the process deeper. For example, if he'd asked about the couple's stories, he might have learned something about their pasts that would have helped him understand why they criticized him as a pastor. Maybe they'd had a bad experience at a previous church where a pastor truly was a my-way-or-the-highway sort of guy and so they were supersensitive about that.

The invitation to sit down and hear people's concerns helps them calm down and be more objective. But the key is listening to them, not defending yourself.

Some people might say they're forgiving, but when they really need to forgive, they don't. As Christians, we need to walk the talk. James 1:22–27 says:

> But be doers of the word, and not hearers only, deceiving yourselves. For if anyone is a hearer of the word and not a doer, he is like a man who looks intently at his natural face in a mirror. For he looks at himself and goes away and at once forgets what he was like. But the one who looks into the perfect law, the law of liberty, and perseveres, being no hearer who forgets but a doer who acts, he will be blessed in his doing.

1. Ravi Zacharias, *I, Isaac, Take Thee, Rebekah: Moving from Romance to Lasting Love* (Nashville: Thomas Nelson, 2004), 25.

If anyone thinks he is religious and does not bridle his tongue but deceives his heart, this person's religion is worthless. Religion that is pure and undefiled before God the Father is this: to visit orphans and widows in their affliction, and to keep oneself unstained from the world. (ESV)

When someone has been wounded, the path to peace starts with a heart for God that leads to a heart for others that leads to a process for making peace.

The Path of Peacemaking

Let's look at the process of peacemaking one more time. After we invite the other person to have a conversation, we do the following:

- Tell our stories together.
- Ascend by praying and reading Scripture together.
- Reflect by taking personal responsibility.
- Connect by asking, confessing, seeking, and forgiving.

Will it be simple? It seldom is.
Will it go just as we hope? It seldom does.
Will we regret trying to be a peacemaker? Never.
We will have created an opportunity in our lives to glorify God.

"We are all faced with a series of great opportunities brilliantly disguised as impossible situations," said Chuck Swindoll.[2] God doesn't have "impossible" in his dictionary.

2. Charles R. Swindoll, *Man to Man: Chuck Swindoll Selects His Most Significant Writings for Men* (Grand Rapids: Zondervan, 1996), 89.

A couple came to my office seeking help. They fought like cats and dogs, so I introduced them to the path of a peacemaker process. They were intrigued but scared.

"We want to try it, but we're afraid we'll fail," she said.

He nodded his head. "What she said."

"Look, give it a try. Remember to pray together, and then tell your story to gain perspective. Then stop and pray and read Scripture. Next, take personal responsibility. Finally, confess and forgive and plan the future. Story. Ascend. Reflect. Connect."

I went to the door.

"You're leaving?" she said. "I'm afraid we'll mess this up."

Her husband nodded his head again.

"I'll be one office over. Come get me if you need me."

Two hours later, I poked my head in. They hardly noticed me. They were too engaged in the process.

Another couple hours passed. I looked in on them again. They were laughing, crying, talking—but, above all, walking the path of peacemakers.

"Who needs me?" I said with a huge smile on my face.

Their session wound up lasting eight hours! It lifted their marriage to a whole new level. Was everything perfect from that day on? No, like all of us, they hit rough patches. But now they had a better way to tap into the God who is always there. The God who can take broken things and fix them. The God who can change circumstances, perspectives, and hearts. The God who can take a kid with no coordination, no confidence, and a father missing from his home—a kid who later struggled with booze and pride—and make him into a pastor and director of an international organization that exists to make peace.

He beckons us to find courage to replace our fear, confidence to replace our white-knuckle worry, and hope to replace our hopelessness. Whether we are in the twilight of our lives and have blown it too many times to count or are young, immature, and unsteady on our feet, the call is the same. Peace is possible if, at first, we connect with the Peacemaker himself.

"But," someone will protest, "it's too late for us. There's no way we can end the war we've been fighting. There might have been a chance if we'd heard about this process long ago but certainly not now." To this I offer an adage from nature. The best time to plant a tree was fifty years ago. The second-best time is now. Right now.

Connect with **Brian Noble** at
www.peacemaker.training

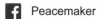 Peacemaker |  @PMministries | @peacemakerministries

@peacemakerministries | Peacemaker Ministries

Connect with

Relevant. Intelligent. Engaging.

Sign up for announcements about
new and upcoming titles at

www.bakerbooks.com/signup

f ReadBakerBooks

y ReadBakerBooks